資産を作る!
資産を防衛する!
「心乱」の投資術

Make assets!
Defend your assets!

Learning investment techniques from failed experiences
My "Trial and Error" investment skills

経営者に不可欠な ファイナンス力（財務力）	**Financial power that is indispensable to management**

社長力の差は、 ファイナンス力の差	**You can dominate your management by having financial power**

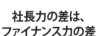

[はじめに]
財テクについて振り返る

財テクで悪いのか？

「オーナー社長のうまみを最大限発揮してどこが悪い!」

　これは、私が若い頃に書いた本のキャッチコピーです(『財テク社長学入門』1989年、大成出版社)。

　今はほぼ死語になりましたが、財務、資金の運用で稼ぐことを「財テク(＝財務テクノロジー)」と言っていました。

　ちなみに、サービス残業の反対語は財テク残業です。お小遣いを稼ぐためにわざと残業をすることをそう言っていました。

　社長は勤勉に稼ぐことも大事、でも稼ぐだけで金持ちになった人は少ない。

「企業成長のテコは財務戦略だ!」

　と、当時はのたまっていたんですね。今では、赤面の至りです(笑)。

[Introduction]
Looking back my financial experience

What's wrong with the fortune-tech?

"What's wrong with maximizing the flavor of owner President!"

This is a catch copy of the book I wrote about when I was young ("Introduction to the President of Technology", Taisei Publishing Company, 1989).

It was almost a dead language now, but it said, "Fortune technology" is to make money by the operation of finance and money (zaitec).

By the way, the opposite word for service overtime is the fortune-tech overtime. In order to earn money, he said to do overtime work

資産の防衛

　それから、20数年過ぎました。
　でも、今こそ、経営者にとって財務力の強化は真に不可欠だと私は再認識しています。
　今の時代は、ファイナンスの時代です。ファイナンスの知識なくして、企業の収益力のアップは考えられません。
　そして、御社の資産防衛、社長個人の資産防衛、商品の開発、どれをとってもファイナンス抜きでは成り立たなくなりました。

on purpose. We called it "zaitec zangyou" in Japanese.

"The president is diligent in his earning, but few people became rich only by their earnings. Corporate growth is a financial strategy!"

I used to write such comments. Now I blush at them.

Asset Defense

20 years have passed since then.

But now, I am re-recognizing that strengthening financial strength is truly essential for business leaders.

Today is the age of finance. Without the knowledge of finance, it is not possible to increase the profitability of a company.

Further, the asset defense of your company, the president's personal assets, development of the product, none of which is able to exist

資産を作ること、増やすこと

さらに言えば、単に資産を防衛だけではおもしろくありません。資産を増やす、これもこの本のテーマにしたいと思います。

えらそうに書きましたが、私の財務の歴史は赤点そのものです。でも、最近は学習効果でだいぶ成果が上がってきました。

そんな私自身の体験を踏まえた原稿になっております。

私は、いいと思ったことをまず自分で始めてみます。ですから、失敗も多くしました。そんな懺悔の本でもあります。

まあ、気楽に読んで下さい。

生意気にも、英語でも書きました。

英語の先生は、『Entrepreneurship 101/失敗から学ぶ起業学入門』の時と同じ、ドアーン先生です。私のオリジナルの英語はズタズタに直されています（笑）。

東峰書房の出口雅人さんにはいつもながら、お世話になりま

without finance.

Increase and create assets

In addition, the defense is not just interesting. I would like to increase my assets, which is also the theme of this book.

This book is never about my pride. My financial history is in the reds. But recently, it has improved significantly with expertise.

It is a manuscript based on such experience.

I want to inform you based on my experience. My investment policy is that at first I will try them and after that, inform you about them.

I appreiciate you who is willing to read my poorly-written English book.

Mr. Duane Walker, my English teacher, helped to correct my previous book (i.e. "Entrepreneurship 101". My original English

した。

　また、売れない拙著をお使いいただいています読者の皆さんにも、この場をお借りして深く御礼申し上げます。

　　　　　　　　　　　　　　2017年6月　　本郷孔洋

has been torn to shreds (laughs).

Thank you Duane sensei! He revised my poor English completely.

I was always indebted to Mr. Masato Deguchi of Tohoshobo.

Also, thank you very much to my readers who will read this poorly-sold book!

June/ 2017   Yoshihiro Hongo

資産を作る! 資産を防衛する!
目次

- はじめに　財テクについて振り返る ——————— 2

++

第1章
体験から導き出したファイナンス力を高めるための必須条件!

1. 両利きの経営
　経営とファイナンス力 ——————————— 18

2. 刷り込み
　人間は賢くない動物、ファイナンス力を高める前に —— 30

3. ファイナンス脳に切り替える
　脳みそは使えば増える、お金は使えば減る ——————— 38

4. お金持ちの定義
　キャッシュフローを多く持っている人 ——————— 44

5. ファイナンス力の必要条件
　何をやるか、方向性が大事 ——————————— 52

6. 逆張り
　これが一番難しい ——————————————— 60

7. 義理を欠いても損はするな!
　投資の心構え ————————————————— 72

Make assets!   Defend your assets!

Table of Contents

- Introduction   Looking back my financial experience —— 3

++

Chapter 1
Essential conditions for increasing financial strength derived from my experience!

1. **Both-handed management and financial strength** —— 19

2. **Imprinting**
   Humans are not wise animals, before increasing your financial strengthstrength —— 31

3. **Turn on your financial brain**
   The more money you spend, the more money lose. On the other hand, when you use your brain more, your brain power increases - you become smarter —— 39

4. **Definition of people**
   Wealthy people have a lot of cash flow in the future —— 45

5. **Financial requirements**
   What you do, and direction is important —— 53

6. **Going against the trend**
   This is the hardest thing! —— 61

7. **Don't let friendship get in the way of profit** —— 73

8. 損する忍耐より儲ける忍耐
株の相場の見方 ———————————— 82

9. 税金
手取りはなんぼか? ———————————— 88

10. 経営者は、B/Sに着目せよ!
財務力はB/S力 ———————————— 96

11. 本郷流投資の考え方
心乱(試行錯誤)の投資術(笑) ———————————— 108

++

第2章
鳥の眼・虫の眼・魚の眼　その①私の鳥の眼　マクロの眼

1. シムズ理論
最後はインフレ ———————————— 120

2. トマ・ピケティ理論
資本収益率(r)は経済成長率(g)よりも常に大きい! ———— 126

3. 私の見立て
2つの理論を踏まえて ———————————— 132

8. Patience to earn more than that to bear a loss ———— 83

9. Tax
How much do you get to keep? ———— 89

10. Pay attention to the B/S!
Financial Power is B/S power ———— 97

11. Under the Hongo Method
My investments of Trial and Error (laughs) ———— 109

++

Chapter 2
Bird eye, insect eye, fish eye ①My bird eye, macro eyes

1. The Sims Theory
Ultimately, inflation ———— 121

2. Thomas Pikketty Theory
The capital return rate (R) is always greater than
the economic growth rate (G)! ———— 127

3. My opinion
Based on two theories ———— 133

++

第3章

鳥の眼・虫の眼・魚の眼　その②私の虫の眼　実践の眼

1. 一通貨二金利
同じ通貨でも国によって金利が違う ———————— 148

2. 短期の延長が長期!
長期の中の短期ではない ———————— 160

3. 定期預金より銀行株
金利よりも配当 ———————— 166

4. 利は元にあり
安く仕入れる ———————— 172

5. 100%のパフォーマンスを求めない
名人、天井売らず底買わず! ———————— 176

6. 休日でも稼げる商売
太陽光投資 ———————— 182

++

第4章

鳥の眼・虫の眼・魚の眼　その③私の魚の眼　流れを読む眼

1. 第2のリーマンショックが来るか?
銀行から政府へ ———————— 198

2. 不動産投資
民泊解禁 ———————— 202

++

Chapter 3
Bird eye, insect eye, fish eye   ②My insect eye, micro eyes

1. **US dollar has two different interest rates though the same currency** ——————— 149

2. **A long-term investment is not necessary** ——————— 161

3. **Bank stock is much better than bank deposits**
   Dividends are much higher than interest rates ——— 167

4. **Profit depends on purchase price** ——————— 173

5. **Don't ask for 100% performance**
   Super Investment Specialist : "Do not buy at the lowest price, and sell before it reaches the the ceiling!" ——— 177

6. **A business to make money even when on holiday**
   Solar Investment ——————————————— 183

++

Chapter 4
Bird eye, insect eye , fish eye
③My fish eye, the eye for of reading change in flow

1. **Is the second Lehman shock coming?** ——————— 199

2. **Real estate investment** ——————— 203

第1章

体験から導き出した ファイナンス力を 高めるための 必須条件!

Chapter 1

Essential conditions
for increasing financial strength derived
from my experience!

1. 両利きの経営
経営とファイナンス力

ファイナンス力

　経営者、ビジネスリーダーは、経営をちゃんとやるのはもちろん重要ですが、ファイナンス力（＝財務力。以下、ファイナンス力）をつけることも必要です。

　いわば経営とファイナンス力、両利きの経営が求められる時代です。

Chapter 1 Essential conditions for increasing financial strength derived from my experience!

1.
Both-handed management and financial strength

Business leaders not only do well in business but also think about finance.

Financial Power

Management and business leaders are, of course, expending their time on management. It is also necessary to put in effort towards financial power.

It is an age when management and finance power as well as both-handed management are demand.

アメリカの一人勝ちの理由

　私の個人的意見ですが、リーマンショックの後に真の21世紀が到来したと思っています。

　完全にカジノ資本主義（＝Casino Capitalism）*化しましたね。リアル経済から金融経済へ完全に移行しました。

　リーマンの後、なぜアメリカが一人勝ちしたか？

　私のシロート判断ですが、バーナンキFRB議長（当時）が、「いち早く金融緩和してお金をばら撒いたからだ」と思っています*。

＊カジノ資本主義（＝Casino Capitalism）

　S.ストレンジが1986年に著した本のタイトルとしても用いられている。20世紀後半における変動相場制への移行や、各国金融の自由化、国際化などによる金融取引の活発化と量的な拡大、金融リスクの増大とキャピタルゲインを含む金融面での収益率の増加が、マネー・ゲームを活発に行なわせるようになり、あたかも密室の中でのギャンブルのように実体経済と

The reason for the US being the sole winner!

Personally, I think the true 21st century came after the Lehman shock.

You've totally made it to casino capitalism*. There was a complete shift from the real economy to the financial economy.

Why did the United States win alone after Lehman?

It is my amateur decision, but the chairman of the Fed Bernanke (at the time) eased money a lot*.

* Casino Capitalism

It is also used as the title of the book that S. Strange wrote in 1986. In the latter half of the 21st century, the increase in financial risk and the growth of capital gains, including the expansion of financial transactions by the liberalization of international financial

は乖離したところで金融活動が行なわれていることから、カジノ資本主義と呼んだ。(「ブリタニカ国際大百科事典 小項目事典」より)

＊もう一つアメリカが日本と違うのは、人口が増えていることなんですね。

つまり、成熟国でありながら、新興国の側面があります。

ですから、インフレになり易い。

そういう意味では、日本のように成熟して、人口減ですと金融政策が立てにくいです(あくまで、シロート判断です。悪しからず)。

institutions, and the growth and quantitative growth of revenue contributed to an activation of the money game and it came to be called casino capitalism because financial activity took place in a closed area much like in a gambling room outside of the real economy. (Encyclopedia Britannica)

* The difference between the United States and the Japan is that the US population is increasing.

The US is a mature country, but it has aspects of an emerging country. Therefore, it becomes privy to inflation.

In that sense, it is difficult to set up a monetary policy in a country like Japan, where the country is mature but has decreasing population. (This is my opinion as an amateur)

アベノミクス

　2012年から始まったアベノミクスで、黒田緩和が行われました。

　私は、これで土地も株もあがりましたし、日本経済は浮上した*と思っています。

　いろいろ反対意見もありますが（笑）。

＊景気回復、戦後３位

　景気動向指数をみると、第二次安倍政権が発足した12年12月に始まった景気回復は17年３月までで52ヶ月になった。バブル景気を抜いた。

　戦後３番目の長さで、今年９月まで回復すると、65年11月―70年７月の57ヶ月間に及んだ「いざなぎ景気」も抜く。(「日本経済新聞」2017年4月7日号より)

Abenomics

In Japan, Abenomics began from December 2012, at which time Mr. Kuroda, the chairman of the Japan Central Bank, also helped to ease financial stress by introducing more money into the economy.

As a result, land and stock prices went up which contributed to the recovery of the Japanese economy*……. Although there were a lot of opposing views to this.

* Economic recovery, third place after the war

Looking at the economic trend index, the economic recovery, which began in December of the second Abe government, lasted for 52 months until March, 2017. Its level of recovery exceeded that of the bubble period economy.

If the economy continues to recover until

ファイナンス力を磨くために

　仮にですよ、事業で勝って、財務で負ける。そういった事態が起こり得る可能性も考えて下さい。

　例えば、1億円の営業利益を出しました。でも、ライバル会社がファイナンス力で10億円稼ぐかもしれないのです。

　これからの経営者にはファイナンスの力をつけることも必要不可欠です。

September of this year, it will also exceed the level of recovery achieved during the "emergency economy -Izanagi keiki", which spanned for a period of 57 months from November, 1965 -July, 1970, in a timeframe of the third longest period of recovery after the World War 2.(from the April 7, 2017 issue of the Japan Economic Newspaper- Nikkei Shimbun)

The difference made possible by finance

Think about the possibility of winning in business and losing in finance.

For example, the operating income can come out to 100 million yen but a rival company could earn 1 billion yen through financial power.

It is essential for business leaders to develop financial strength.

ファイナンスの差

まず、興味を持たないとダメです。

言うは易しです。なぜなら、これは、日本的カルチャーへの挑戦だからです。

生来、日本では、ひたいに汗して稼いだお金でなければ、不浄なお金でしたからね。

しかし、時代は変わりました。

ですから、ビジネス成功のためには、そのトレンドに乗ることが、とても重要だと思うんです。

How to hone your financial power

First of all, you have to be interested in finance.

It's easier said than done, because it's a challenge to Japan culture.

In Japan, money used to have to be earned by gaining sweat on your forehead.

But times have changed.

Therefore, I think it is very important to ride the trend in order to succeed in business.

2.

刷り込み
人間は賢くない動物、ファイナンス力を高める前に

土地神話の崩壊

　戦後からバブル崩壊まで、土地はずっと値上がりしていました。

　株も、土地ほど一本調子ではありませんが、やはり持っていれば値上がりしました。

　その頃、会社の決算書を見て、現金しか持っていない会社があれば、不遜にも、「なんで土地買わないの？」なんて社長に意見していました（恥ずかしい（笑））。

　それが、バブル崩壊です。

2.

Imprinting

Humans are not wise animals, before increasing your financial strength

I feel that people are not suited for changes in the economic environment.

Let's look at some mistakes I made in the past.

The collapse of the land myth

After World War 2, land prices began to rise, the land myth "Tochi-shinwa" – meaning that, if we bought real estate, its value would increase forever. But, of course, that did not happen.

The stock is not as good as land, but if you had one, its value appreciated.

During that time, I wrongfully

土地が下がるなんて信じられませんでしたね。

土地神話の後遺症

　正直、バブルの崩壊後もいつかは土地の価格が戻ると信じていました。

　私だけではありません。友人で土地の価格が下がった時、チャンスとばかり、また土地を買って傷口を広げた人もいました。

　デフレがくるという意見もあったんですよ。

　でも、人間は謙虚に他人の意見に耳を傾ける動物ではないんですね。

　私の経験では、あたまで理解1年、腹オチ10年ですかね。

　定かではありませんが、「これはホントにデフレなんだ」と真に腹オチしたのは、10年以上は過ぎていましたね。

　「あたま1年、からだ10年」

recommended land purchase to clients who owned only cash in assets. I am so embarrassed.

When the Japanese bubble economy collapsed in early 1992, the land myth "Tochi-shinwa" also collapsed.

I couldn't believe the land was going down.

The aftermath of the land myth

I was positive that land prices would surely rise again. I never imagined that deflation would continue over the next 20 years.

When real estate prices decreased, a friend of mine thought this would be a good opportunity for buying property. However, real estate prices decreased further and further.

There was also an opinion that deflation would come. Human beings are not wise animals (laughs).

人間って賢くない動物です（笑）。

　人間が賢くない動物であることを言い聞かせながらファイナンスを学ぶ、これが私の体験からつくづく思うことです。

あたまでは解っていても……

　バブル崩壊後、私も手持ちの不動産を売るのに躊躇しました。それで長い間借金を返すのに四苦八苦しましたね。

　その時、考えました。今の事業規模では借金の返済は無理だ、と思ったのですね。それで、売り上げを増やし、相対的に借金の比率を下げようと思いました。

　それが、業容拡大に繋がり、会計事務所もソコソコ大きな規模にすることができました。だから、結果的にかえって良かったのかな？

I couldn't understand this opinion at that time.

I understand this in 1 year and truly understood it only after 10 years.

I know from experience that you should always know that humans are not smart, when going through the process of learning about finances.

Even if you know in your brain……

I hesitated to sell my real estate. Therefore, I struggled to repay my debts for a long time.

At that time, I thought at the current scale of business, it was impossible to repay the debt. So, I wanted to increase sales and lower the debt ratio relatively.

It was connected to the expansion of the business, and my accounting business has become relatively large scale.

So, was it a good result?

「刷り込み」が捨てられるか！

　とまれ、財務力を高めるなどという技術の前に、この気持ちがとても大切ですね。

　後述する魚の眼が磨けません（第 4 章参照）。

"Imprinting" can be discarded!

This feeling is very important before the technology of increasing financial strength.

If you don't discard imprinting, you cannot polish the eyes of the fish to be described later.

3.

ファイナンス脳に切り替える

脳みそは使えば増える、お金は使えば減る

ファイナンス脳

　理屈っぽくいいますと、経営をお金という観点で見ると速習できるのではないでしょうか？

　ビジネスでも経営者の考え方次第で、大きく変えることは可能です。

　要するに「ファイナンス脳」に切り替え、磨くことなんですね。

　私は、上場会社に時価総額があるように、自社の企業価値を絶えず金銭評価することが近道だと思うんですね。

Chapter 1 Essential conditions for increasing financial strength derived from my experience!

> # 3.
>
> # Turn on your financial brain
>
> The more money you spend, the more money lose. On the other hand, when you use your brain more, your brain power increases - you become smarter

Financial Brain

If you want to quickly hone your financial brain, you should see management in terms of money.

If business leaders decide to change their mindset, their business strategy will also change.

In short, turn on the financial brain and hone it.

I think it's a shortcut to constantly evaluate the money value of your company, so that the

P/L脳からB/S脳へ

損益思考も大事ですが、これがP/L（損益計算書）脳だとすれば、B/S（バランスシート）脳を磨くことも大事なんですね。

例えば、M&Aしたい会社があったとします。

「お金がない」であきらめないで、どうしたら、それが買えるか？

こんな脳の切り替えでも、グンとファイナンス力が付きます。

買った会社のキャッシュフローで買えるかどうか（LBO）、とか。

お金が私のために働いているのだ！

「私はお金のために働いているのではない、お金が私のために働いているのだ！」

listed companies have "market capitalization".

From P/L brain to B/S brain

Thinking about profit and loss is important, but this is not only a P/L (income statement) brain, it is also important to polish brain in terms of B/S (balance sheet).

For example, suppose you have a company that wants to be M&A.

Don't give up on "having no money!" You should always think "how you can buy it?"

Even turning on your brain, allows finance power.

Maybe you can buy it with the cash flow of the company to be acquired(LBO).

Money is working for me!

"I'm not working for money, the money is working for me! "

「お金のために働くのではなく、お金を自分のために働かせる」（『金持ち父さん貧乏父さん』ロバート・キヨサキ著、シャロン・レクター著、白根美保子訳、2000年、筑摩書房）

　ここまできますと、ファイナンス力は、達人の域？（笑）

"Make money work for yourself, not for money"

This is "Robert T. Kiyosaki's quote" from his best selling book, ("Rich Dad, Poor dad"by Robert Kiyosaki).

If we come this far, are we financial gurus?

第1章 体験から導き出したファイナンス力を高めるための必須条件!

4.
お金持ちの定義
キャッシュフローを多く持っている人

現金はお金を生みません

　モノの価値は「将来生み出すキャッシュフローの総額」です。
　「ファイナンス的な意味でのお金持ちといのうは、キャッシュフローを生む資産を多く持っている人である」(『あれか、これか―「本当の値打ち」を見抜くファイナンス理論入門』野口真人著、ダイヤモンド社、2016年)
　私もまったく同意見です。
　金融的に言いますとキャッシュを生まない土地は価値がありません。
　たとえ大地主でも、有効利用しない、キャッシュを生まない土地をいくら持っていても価値がないのです。

4.
Definition of people
Wealthy people have a lot of cash flow in the future

Cash doesn't make money

The value of properties is the sum of the cash flow to be created in the future.

("The introduction of finance theory" to see "real value", the wealthy people in a financial sense have many assets that generate cash flow. Diamond Company, Mahito Noguchi)

I agree with this.

The land that does not give birth to cash does not have value.

Landowners, who do not make use of their land effectively, do not make a profit and their land has no value.

自社株もキャッシュ化の時代

「息子さんは、あなたの株をノーサンキュウ！」

すごく売れたキャッチです。

なるほどなーと思いました。

評価の高い自社株式を相続するのは大変です。後継者は、換金されない株のために多大な借金をして相続します。それを何十年にも渡って返済します。

こんなことバカくさい、と思う後継者も現れるでしょうね。

私見ですが、自社株もキャッシュ化の時代が来ますね。

経営と資本が分離する時代、資本がなくても、経営の継続ができる時代が来るような気がします。

You should cash your company's stock

Your son do not appreciate your stock!

This is the very popular catch phrase.

I understand this situation very well⋯.

This is because the successor can't easily convert stock to cash. It is difficult to inherit a highly valued company stock. The successor owes a great deal of debt for the stock that is not cashed.

It has to be repaid it for decades.

My personal opinion is that the age of cash-making stock will come. Even if the successor has no capital.

I feel that the age of separated management and capital will come.

P/Lは損益、B/Sはキャッシュフロー

　6月は株主総会のシーズンです。つくづく、上場会社の経営者は、大変だなと思います。

　長期的利益を犠牲にしても、短期的利益を追求しなければなりませんから。

「長期的投資は、キャッシュを生むことが条件」です。

　言い換えますと、

「お金持ちとは、キャッシュフローを多く持っている人です」（同書より）

長期的利益と短期的利益

　単純に言いますと、P/Lは損益で、B/Sはキャッシュフローです。

　いくら当期利益で頑張っても、長期のキャッシュを生む元を削っては意味がありません。

P/L is profit and loss. B/S is cash flow

June is the shareholders meeting season. I think that business leaders of listed companies are very serious.

They have to pursue a short term profit. As a result, they may lose long term profit.

"A long term investment is a condition that can generate cash".

In other words,

"Sucessful companies have a lot of cash flow over a long term".

Long term profit and short term profit

Simply put, P/L is profit and loss, and B/S is cash flow.

You shouldn't cut back on your original long term investment (for profit).

理想的には、経営者は短期的にも長期的にも対応する、両利きの経営が理想です。

私の失敗体験
（でも、キャッシュフローで救われた）

私の経験でも、投資の基準は、将来のキャッシュフローがポイントです。

昔、バブルの時、私も不動産でだいぶ損をしました。

でも、救われた理由として、不動産の家賃収入がありました。

一方、値上がり期待で買ったゴルフの会員権は、紙くずになるし配当もありません。

その時、長期的な投資は、やはりキャッシュフローがキモだなとつくづく思ったものでした。

Ideally, management needs both long and short-term profit.

My failure
(but I saved my cash flow)

My experience is that investment standards are the point of future cash flow.

In the past, during the bubble, I lost a lot in real estate.

But the reason I was saved was that real estate had rental income.

On the other hand, I bought a membership at a golf club, with the expectation of a price hike. But the membership became scrap paper, and there was no dividend either.

At that time, I really thought that long term investments were to enable cash flow for the future.

第1章 体験から導き出したファイナンス力を高めるための必須条件!

5.
ファイナンス力の必要条件
何をやるか、方向性が大事

私の経験

①お金儲けのうまい人の必要条件は2つかな?

・努力できることが才能

・努力には方向性がある

②「努力できることが才能である 」

これは、松井秀喜が言って有名になった言葉です。

本人の記念館(松井秀喜ベースボールミュージアム)に掲げてあるそうです。松井のお父さんが、紙に書いて松井に渡し、それ以降、松井は自分の部屋に貼っていたそうです。

資産形成は、コツコツとした継続的努力が必要です。

決めたことをちゃんと継続的に実行できる能力です。

Chapter 1 Essential conditions for increasing financial strength derived from my experience!

5.
Financial requirements
What you do, and direction is important

From my experience

There are two requirements for a skillful person to make money.

① They have an ability to make an effort, and also not to mistake the direction of the effort.

②"It is a talent to be able to make an effort".
This is the phrase that Hideki Matsui became famous for.
It is listed in the Baseball Memorial Hall (Matsui Hideki Baseball Museum). Matsui's father wrote it on paper and handed it to his son, and after that, Matsui hung it in his room.

③継続的努力

　言い換えますと、資産形成には継続的努力が不可欠です。

　商売のうまい人はたくさんいます。でもどうでしょう、商売がうまいと同時に金持ちなった人は少数です。

　これは、才能の差というより、継続的努力の差ではないかと思っています。

　長い間お金持ちを見てきましたが、まずこれがないとだめですね。

　当たり前ですが、貯めるはガマン、使うは一瞬です。

④「努力には方向性がある」

　孟子が言ったとされる、私の大好きな言葉です。

　松井選手は、有名選手になっただけでなく、なぜ、大金持ちになったのでしょう？

Acquiring assets requires a continuous effort.

This is the ability to carry out the decisions properly and continuously.

③ Continuous effort

To paraphrase, continuous effort is essential for asset acquisition.

There are a lot of skillful people in business. But, there are few people who are good at business and wealthy at the same time.

I think that this is not a difference of talent but a difference of ongoing effort.

I have seen wealty people for a long time.

If you want to be wealty, you should make an ongoing effort.

④People have the ability to make an effort, and also not to mistake the direction of the effort.

"Direction is important".

私はセミナーでたまにこの質問をします。

　大概の回答は、「努力したから」あるいは「大変才能があったから」です。

　正解は、「野球をやったから」です。

　一流選手になったのは努力と才能によりますが、それだけでは大金持ちになりません。

　ホントの正解は、彼らは野球という稼げる職業を選び、大リーグという日本より稼げる場所で活躍したからなんですね。

　他のスポーツでは、いくら才能があって、努力して、一流選手になったとしても、こうはいきません。

　金メダルをとった人は数えきれないほどいますが、そのうち何人が金持ちになったんでしょうか？

"Effort has direction".

Mencius said this. It is my favorite phrase.

Not only did Matsui become a famous baseball player, he also became a millionaire.

How?

I ask this question once in a while in my seminar.

Most of the answers are "because he tried and he was very talented".

However, the correct answer is "because he played baseball".

Becoming a leading player takes talent and effort, but it does not guarantee becoming a millionaire.

The real answer is that he chose a lucrative career in baseball, and that's because he worked in a place (Major League Baseball) where he could earn more money than playing in the Japan big leagues.

In other sports, no matter how talented, challenging, and successful, there are few

athletes who can earn a lot of money.

The number of people who won gold medals is countless, but how many of them became wealthy?

6.

逆張り
これが一番難しい

不景気と設備投資

昔から、有能な経営者は、不景気の時に設備投資をしました。
理由は、安く作れるからです。
投資も同じです。

「麦わら帽子は冬に買え」

相場の格言です。でもこれができないのが人間でもあります。
故事に学ぶとすれば、J・F・ケネディのお父さん*の神話でしょうか?

6.
Going against the trend
This is the hardest thing!

Recession and capital expenditures

A long time ago, some smart business leaders invested in capital during the recession.

It was a good opprtunity to invest cheaply.

Finacial investment is the same.

"You can buy straw hats in winter"

This is a general rule of the stock market. But we cannot usually do that.

Do you know the myth of J. F. Kennedy's

靴磨きでさえ株をやってると、暴落前に株を売り抜けた故事ですね。

　でも、マレですから、故事として残るんですよね(笑)。

「犬が人を噛んでもニュースにならないが、人が犬を噛むとニュースになる」

　このマスコミのたとえの通り行動する。

　できるかな？(笑)

＊ジョセフ・パトリック・"ジョー"・ケネディ・シニア（Joseph Patrick "Joe" Kennedy, Sr.、1888年9月6日 － 1969年11月18日）はアメリカ合衆国の政治家・実業家、第35代大統領のジョン・F・ケネディの父である。

　1929年の大暴落の時、ジョーは暴落を予期して直前にほとんどの株を売り払っていたため、被害を受けなかった。よく彼の慧眼を示すエピソードとして「ウォール街で靴を磨いていたパット・ボローニャなる男までが株式取引に精通しているのを見

father*?

There is a story about him selling all his stocks before the stock market crashed.

One day he was having his shoes polished by a shoeshine boy.

That boy asked him about the stock market.

"Even a shoeshine boy had bought stock!"

He was worried if the stock market would crash.

"If a dog bites a person, it won't be news, but it's a big news when a person bites a dog."

It is a general rule of media.

* Joseph Patrick "Joe" Kennedy Senior (Joseph Patrick "Joe" Kennedy, Mower, September 6, 1888-November 18, 1969, is the father of the United States politician, businessman and John F. Kennedy of the 35th president.

During the great Crash of 1929, Joe was not harmed because he had sold most of his shares just before he anticipated the crash. Well as

て、株式市場はそろそろ危ないと気づいた」という話がなされるが、これはジョーの作り話であるといわれ、実際にはパトロンのガイ・カリアの「株式市場はそろそろ危ない」という忠告に従ったものだったといわれている。(「Wikipedia」より)

人生にビックチャンスは、2、3度ある

　よく言われることですが、人生には、ビックチャンス（金儲け、ビジネス等）が2、3度あるといわれています。

　これは、私の経験でもよくわかります。

　これは、いつも言っているのですが、ノーハウよりノーフーです。誰と出会ったか？

　自分の人生を振り返っても、そう思うんですね。大きな出会いは2、3度ありました。

　悩ましいのは、気づくのは後付けなんですね。私もそうでし

an episode showing his insight (cervical) "I saw a guy who was polishing shoes on Wall Street to be a pat Bologna who was familiar with stock trading, and I realized that the stock market is about to be dangerous". It is said that this is Joe's fiction, and it is actually the one that the patron's moth Lee Kalia's "stock market is soon dangerous" according to the advice. (from Wikipedia)

There are a couple of big chances in life

It is often said that there are a few big chances in life, such as making money and doing business.

I understand this very well because of my past experiences.

I think if you want to make chances for yourself, it's not what you know; it's who you know. In other words, by meeting skillful

た。

　大半の人は、多分そのチャンスがあっても、気づかないかで過ぎ去ってしまいます。でも、そのチャンスだって、せいぜい人生２、３度です。

　でも、私の場合、運が良かったのか、その出会いが次のステップに繋がったんですね。

　若い人にアドバイスするとすれば、「執念を持て」ですかね。目の前のいい出会いを、淡白にやり過ごすことかな？

　それで、みすみすいい出会いをなくしてしまう。

　もったいない！

people we can have the opportunity to change our lifes.

When I look back on my life, I agree with this. There were a few big encounters.

Unfortunately, we usually can't recognize a good chance when it arises.

For most people, when a chance appears, it will not be noticed. Perhaps, after some time we will recognize this as a good chance, but by then it's already too late.

In my case, I was lucky, and the encounter led to the next step.

If you have the opportunity for a good meeting, you should take it.

お金に定年はない　稼げた人から稼ぎ続ける人になるために

ビジネスには、定年があります。

会社の定年はもとより、個人経営でも、旬は短いですね。

でも、お金には定年がありません。もっと言いますと、死すらありません。007の様に。お金は永遠に不滅です（笑）。

「モテた人は多いのですが、モテ続ける人は少ない」

私ぐらいの年になりますと、過去のモテた同じ話を何回も聞きます。

過去の彼女の写真を後生大事に持っている人もいて、何回

Money does not mean retirement. Don't be a person who earns temporarily. Be a person who continuously makes money!

Business has a retirement age.

There is retirement age in companies, and also in individual management. Working life is short.

However, money does not have a retirement age. Money will never die, just like James Bond (007). Money is immortal (laughs).

There are many people who are popular, but few people can continue to be popular

I'm old and my classmates are also old. There are some people who were very popular in the past.

My classmates are very proud to tell the

も同じ写真を見せられます。でも、相手ももうおばあちゃんなんだろうなと想像します。
「おもしろうてやがて悲しき鵜飼かな」
　人生はピークがあるんだなーとつくづく思いますね。
　ところで、自分の事業にも波があります。というよりピークは一瞬です。
　稼いだ人は多いのですが、稼ぎ続ける人は少ないのです。稼げた人から稼ぎ続ける人になるために、ファイナンスが登場します。
　そのためには、お金の力が不可欠です。
　繰り返し言います。
「お金は永遠に不滅です!」
「読売巨人軍は永遠に不滅です」(笑)。

same stories every time we meet. Some people have cherished photographs from the past, and many times the same photo is shown.

"At first, it's very funny, but it's a sad later if we see cormorant game"

This is an ancient legend.

I really think that life has its peak. By the way, there is also a wave in our business- the peak moment.

There are a lot of people who make money, but there are few who can keep making money. We have to be in a situation where our money naturally makes more money.

Therefore, the power of money is indispensable.

Say it again.

"Money is immortal! "

"The Yomiuri Giants are immortal" (laughs).

第1章 体験から導き出したファイナンス力を高めるための必須条件!

7.
義理を欠いても損はするな!
投資の心構え

①「ドクターには義理を欠いてもいい」

と、いう言い伝えがあります(ホントかな(笑))。

現実的には、世話になっているドクター先生に義理を欠くわけですから、とても勇気がいりますが。

でも、自分の命は自分で守らなければなりません。

「悪いと思わないこと」です。

私も、「ドクターを代えたらいいのに」というケースを間近に見ています。最低でも、セカンドオピニオンは、自分の命を守るためには不可欠です。

Chapter 1 Essential conditions for increasing financial strength derived from my experience!

7.
Don't let friendship get in the way of profit

"Protect your life even if your doctor is a friend"

"This is an ancient legend"

It's a joke (laughs).

Try not to feel obligated to your doctor-it's your life and you should be responsible for it.

Sometimes it's necessary to seek a second opinion in order to protect ourselves-especially in regards to health.

②絶対に損をする

　ウォーレンバフェットの語録の中に次のような言葉があります。

　ルールその1：絶対に損をしないこと。

　ルールその2：「ルールその1」を忘れないこと。

　私の邪推ですが、過去にバフェットさんもずいぶんと損した、人には言えない苦い経験があるんでしょうね。

　これは、私も身に染みました（笑）。

　絶対に損をするのが投資です。

③投資アドバイザーには、義理を欠いてもいい

　税理士と投資アドバイザーには、義理を欠いてもいい！（笑）

　投資の世界もドクターと一緒ではないでしょうか？

　必ず投資を勧めるアドバイザーがいます。付き合っていくうちに仲良くなります。

　すると、しばしば、義理での投資をすることがあります。

Loss is indispensable in investment

These are some of his wise ideas in Warren Buffett's aphorisms.

Rule 1: Never lose.

Rule 2: Don't forget rule1.

It is my guess that Mr. Buffett has suffered a lot of loses in the past.

He has had bitter experiences that he could not talk to anyone about.

I think investments will definitely make losses over time.

You may lose Investment advisors too

There are always some advisors who recommend investing. We will usually become close friends with them.

でも、失敗すれば、自分の損です。当たり前ですが（笑）。
「義理を欠いても損はしない」鉄則です。

　これは、私の懺悔と体験からのアドバイスです（笑）。

最後はキャッシュ、含み益ほど当てにならないものはない！

「含み益ほど当てにならないものはない」
　これは、ドイツの金融関係者の言い伝えだそうです。
　私もバブルの時、痛いほど経験しました。
　少し株や不動産を買って、値上がりして、知り合いに「いくら含み益がある」なんて自慢しましたから。
　でも崩壊は一瞬でした。株やゴルフの会員権は紙くず同然でした。
　ですから、私の経験でも、やはり最後はキャッシュです。常に現金化できる体制が必要です。
「常に現金化を考えろ！」
　これは、私の投資の基本です。

And you may often invest following their recommendations.

But if they fail, you will lose your money.

You shouldn't lose your investment even if you lose your friends (your advisor).

This is my confession and advice.

Cash is the most reliable property of all

"You never rely on unrealized gains"

This is a legend of German Bankers.

In the bubble period, I had painful experience of this.

At that time, I had small-unrealized gains from some stocks and real estate. My friends were proud of me.

But the bubble suddenly burst. Stocks and golf club memberships were worthless (This is why I think you need a system that you can always cash in on).

それには、魚の眼が不可欠ですが。

エラそうには言えないなー(笑)。

リスク

「富には、リスクが伴う」

これは、中国の言い伝えだそうです。

問題はリスクの範囲です。

トカゲの尻尾＊は30％まで切られても再生するそうです。

孫さんの記事を読んで以来、私は、リスクの範囲を３割と決めています。

単細胞ですが。

でも、張る金額が多くなりますと、率では変わりませんが、額が多くなります。

ですから、リスクのパーセンテージは変わりませんが、リターンは大きくなります。

You should think about that if something happens-how to cash your properties as soon as possible.

This is the basis of my investments.

It is essential to be adaptible like a fish changing course in a river.

Risk

"You can not become wealthy without risk"

This is a legend of Chinese wealthy people.

There is the range of risk.

The tail of the lizard* is likely to survive even if 30% is cut off.

I have decided that my risk range is 30%, since I read Mr. Son's interview article.

I'm simple! I immediately believed this article.

You can invest more money into your business when you expand. The rate of investment will not change, but the amount

＊トカゲは尻尾切りで有名です。
「自切」といって、自らの体を捨てて、外敵から身を守る。
　さて、何割までが再生可能か?
　ネットを調べたのですが、出て来ませんでした。

of money will be higher.

So you can see that the percentage of the risk will not change, but the return will be greater.

* Lizards are known to cut off their own tail to protect themselves from predators.

Well, what is the percentage of survival?

I checked the Internet, but there was no answer.

8. 損する忍耐より儲ける忍耐
株の相場の見方

「コツコツドカン」

これは象徴的な言葉です。

小さく慎重に稼いで、ドカンとやられる。

これは、経済学というより心理学ですね。

ホントに良くやられました（笑）。

損する忍耐より儲ける忍耐

儲ける時は上昇相場で忍耐強く我慢して大きく値幅を取りにいこうという格言です。

8.
Patience to earn more than that to bear a loss

"Kotsu Kotsu Dokan"

This is a symbolic term.

It means to earn small amounts in a steady fashion, then to lose it all.

This is more related to psychology than economics.

This happened to me many times (laugh).

Patience to earn more than that to bear a loss

It is a well-known maxim in the trade market to endure patiently when the market

これは相場の有名な格言です。

　つまり、

「株は儲からないという投資家の多くは、儲けている投資家と逆のことをしていることが多いようです。複数の銘柄に投資した時の例をあげます。

　値上がりした銘柄、値下がりした銘柄が出た時に個人投資家は値上がりして、わずかな利益が出た銘柄を売り、評価損の銘柄を手元に残します。

　プロの投資家は逆で、上げている銘柄は上昇エネルギーが強いとみて手元に残し、下げている銘柄はいつ回復するかわからない、さらに下値を追うかもしれないという見方をします」

（ネットより）

goes up and wait to obtain a profit under a larger price range.

This is what it means:

"Many of the investors who are not making a profit are doing the opposite of what investors who are making a profit are doing. The following is an example of an instance when investors purchase multiple types of stock.

When the price of certain types of stock go up and that of other types of stock goes down, individual investors will sell the types of stock that bear a small profit, and keep the ones that bear a small valuation loss.

On the contrary, professional investors view this as the types of stock that are going up in price are strong, while the types of stock that are going down in value are weak, and that it is unclear when the types of stock that are going down in value will recover, where there is a possibility that they might

そして、待つ!

　私が過去に一番できなかったことです。

　マージャンで見(ケン)という言葉があります。

　これは、ゲームに参加せず、情勢を見守り、次のゲームの戦略を練ること。一流のマージャンの勝負師はこの能力が高いとされています。(ネットより)

　投資もこれが必要で、これができない人は一流の投資家になれない?

　私はつくづくそう思うんですね。

　ちょっと儲けて、営業マンに薦められて、休まず買う。

　これって、アホか、カモか(苦笑)。

even go lower in price". (from the Internet)

And then, wait!

This was what I couldn't do in the past.

There is a term called (KEN) in mahjong.

This means to not participate in the game, but to observe it and devise a strategy for the next game. First-rate mahjong players are considered to be highly-skilled in this area. (from the Internet)

This is also a necessary skill in investment, where a person who does not exercise this skill is not likely to be able to become a first-rate investor.

Often think, are we stupid in repeating the cycle of making a purchase upon the recommendation of a salesperson, then making a small profit, and then making a purchase again?

第1章 体験から導き出したファイナンス力を高めるための必須条件!

9.
税金
手取りはなんぼか?

「年俸を手取りなんぼくれ」

　昔、プロ野球の有名選手が、「年棒を手取りなんぼくれ」と掛け合ってマスコミにたたかれました。

　でも、これは投資の眼からいいますと、当然の視点です。

　専門書には節税と書かれていますが、別に節税でもなんでもありません。税法通りにやるだけで、有利不利は私たちが判断すればいいだけのことです。

　私のポイントは以下の2点です。

Chapter 1 Essential conditions for increasing financial strength derived from my experience!

9.

Tax

How much do you get to keep?

"Please give me a certain amount of income after tax"

In the old days, professional baseball players were criticized by the press for negotiating the terms of their take-home pay after taxes.

However, this is a legitimate perspective, from an investment point-of-view.

In professional books, this is referred to as "tax savings", but this is not actually tax savings. This is carried out in accordance with the tax rules, as to which we only need to determine if it is beneficial/not beneficial.

I would like to make the following two points.

①法人で投資するか、個人で投資するか?

一長一短です。

短期的投資、長期の投資で、税金が違います。

私は面倒なのであまり税金のことを考えないで大体法人で投資をしています。

プロとして情けないのですが(笑)。

②税目ごとの検討も必要

税の専門用語で税目というのがあります。

資産税なのか、所得税なのか、法人税なのか、単純に税率だけを見ないで、投資目的をよく検討することも不可欠です。

相続を意識した場合、資産税(相続税、贈与税)を中心に検討して下さい。

事業承継対策では、株価評価も大きなポイントになります。

税効果を入れた利回り計算でも、節税効果がなくても回る資産に投資をする

①Do you invest as an individual or a corporation?

They have each advantages and disadvantages.

Tax is different for short-term investment and long-term investment.

I usually invest as a corporation because I would like to not think about taxes too much, and avoid painstaking details.

I am disqualified as a pro (laughs).

②It is also necessary to give consideration to each tax item.

There are some different tax categories for example, asset tax, income tax or corporate tax and so on. It is also essential to consider investment objectives. You should never make a decision based on low tax rate.

If you are aware of an inheritance, consider the asset tax (inheritance tax, gift tax) first.

If we think about business succession, we

卵は一つのカゴで運べ！敢えて、選択と集中せよ！お金には色がある

「卵は一つのカゴで運ぶな！」というリスク分散のことわざがあります。

狡兎三窟*という言葉があります。

私は、「狡兎三窟」の言葉の方が好きでよく使います。

以前、私も資産新3分割法なんて、しゃべっていました。

でも、それだと資産は増えないのですね。

最近では、選択と集中の方がいいのではと思っています。

should focus on price evaluation.

Let's consider your real estate investment. Many real estate brokers include a tax-effective yield in normal yield calculations. However, you should calculate yield without any tax benefits.

Carry all eggs in one basket!

I dare to say you should focus on just one category if you choose investment products.

"Don't carry all your eggs in one basket!"

This is a proverb of risk variance.

In other words, "the rabbit has three burrows*".

I prefer this phrase to "Don't carry all your eggs in one basket!"

There are three-division methods of

＊すばしこいうさぎは３つの隠れ穴をもって危険から身を守るという意味から、身の安全を保つために、いくつかの避難場所や策を用意するたとえ。(ネットより)

assets. It's the right policy.

But if we want to increase our assets, it's just not sufficient.

So recently, I think that it is better to choose and focus on just one product. Recently, I don't use the three-division method for assets. This is because we don't usually have a lot of money to invest. Even if we protect our assets, they will not grow.

*Quick rabbits have three burrows to protect themselves from danger, and to keep them safe, and to prepare some evacuation places and measures. (from the Internet)

10.
経営者は、B/Sに着目せよ!
財務力はB/S力

重要なB/Sの役割

財務戦略には、B/Sのフル活用がとても重要です。

もちろんP/Lで稼ぐことは基本ですが、それだけでは不十分です。

昨今の円安でドル換算しますと、ほとんどの日本企業のB/Sは目減りしました。

言い換えますと、「P/Lで勝って、B/Sで負ける」ということになりました。

10.
Pay attention to the B/S!
Financial Power is B/S power

Key role of B/S

The full use of the B/S is very important for financial strategy.

Of course, it is fundamental to earn in P/L, but that is not enough.

In terms of the recent weakening of the yen, the B/S in most Japanese companies has been reduced.

In other words, "win by P/L and lose by B/S".

M&Aの時代は、財務力がキモ

　また、成熟化時代の成長戦略は、M&A戦略を抜きにして考えられません。

　会社を成長させたい、伸ばしたいと考えるなら、M&Aは不可欠です。M&Aは、B/S重点で考えます。

　例えば、LBO*は、相手の会社の資産のフル活用です。

　買収資金は、相手会社のレバレッジのフル活用です。

　これだって、P/Lというより、自社のB/Sの活用です。

＊LBO（レバレッジド・バイアウト Leveraged Buyout）

　LBOとは、主としてプライベート・エクイティ・ファンドなどが、買収先の資産及びキャッシュフロー（キャッシュ・マネジメント）と自身のジャンク債を担保に負債を調達し、買収した企業の資産の売却や事業の改善などを買収後に行うことによってキャッシュフローを増加させることで負債を返済していくM&A手法である。少ない自己資本で、相対的に大きな資本の企業を買収

Today is the age of M&A, so financial (B/S) power is a key point

Moreover, the growth strategy cannot be thought of without the M&A strategy.

M&A is essential if you want to grow and extend your company.

For example, LBO* uses the full assets of the other company.

Takeover funds can be made by the company to be acquired.

This is the use of B/S rather than P/L.

* Leveraged Buyout

A leveraged buyout (LBO) is a financial transaction in which a company is purchased with a combination of equity and debt, such that the company's cash flow is the collateral used to secure and repay the borrowed money. The use of debt, which has a lower

できることから、梃の原理になぞらえて「レバレッジド・バイアウト」と呼ばれる。（「Wikipedia」より）

経営者はB/S力を磨く

　以上のように、経営者は、稼ぐ力をP/L力とすると、これはもちろんですが、B/S力、つまり財務力を磨くのもとても大切です。
「俺は、カネは苦手だ!」と照れて言う社長さんもおりますが、現在の経営は、それでは不十分です。
　成熟化国家はどうしても、お札増刷社会（金融主体の社会）になります。
　私見で恐縮ですが、良し悪しは別として、経営者の財務力は、自社の成長戦略を左右するといっても過言ではないですね。

cost of capital than equity, serves to reduce the overall cost of financing the acquisition. This reduced cost of financing allows greater gains to accrue to the equity, and, as a result, the debt serves as a lever to increase the returns to the equity. (from Wikipedia)

Business leaders should learn B/S

Business leaders have to learn not only P/L, but also B/S.

"I'm not good with money!"

Many Japanese business leaders often say that. But the current management methods are not enough if business leaders have no idea about money.

The maturing first world nations will become a money-reprint society (financial society).

In my opinion, the financial power of business leaders (apart from the good or

P/Lは足し算、B/Sは掛け算

　労働から生まれる利益はP/Lです。
　逆にB/Sは、「資産によって得られる富」を得ることができます。
　敢えて言いますが、P/Lは足し算ですが、B/Sは、掛け算の成長戦略が取れます。

B/Sの高速回転

　ゼロ金利ですから、B/Sを不稼動にしますと目減りします。
　すると、経常利益にも影響します。受取利息が稼げませんものね。
　そして、ファイナンスは回転数です。回転数次第で、収益力がアップします。出と入りの高速回転が必要です。B/Sの高速回転です。
　B/Sの高速回転による、収益力のサポートは、私は不可欠だと思うんですね（もちろん損するリスクもあります）。

bad strategies), depends on the company's growth strategy.

P/L addition, B/S multiplication

Profit from Labor is P/L.

Conversely, B/S can obtain the wealth gained by assets. I dare to say, you can expand your business by using B/S power.

High-speed B/S rotation

Since it is a zero interest rate, if you make the B/S non-operating, B/S value will decrease.

Also, recurring income may decrease. Of course, you can't earn interest income.

Financial power depends on the number of rotations. This means the number of times you use B/S. You need use B/S at a high

商品開発も金融との合わせ技

ファイナンスの時代は、金余りの時代です。

容易に、しかも低金利で調達できます。

既存の商品をファイナンスと組み合わせて、レンタル商品ができます。

すると、商品をレンタルにすると、商品単品売りより金融利益が自社に取り込めます。

従来、リース会社に渡していた、金融利益が自社に入ります。

営業利益＝金融利益（資産利益）

定年後を豊かにするためには、サラリーマンは、不労所得と

rotation.

If you can make a profit by using B/S, it's much better for your company.

We need a technique to combine product development with finance

The age of finance overflows with money.

Therefore, we can easily borrow money at low interest. You can develop products combined with finance.

Profits can be made not only from existing products but also from financial profit.

For example, when you rent a product, you can get incorporate financial benefits into your company.

Operating income = financial gain (Asset profit)

In order to enrich the retirement age,

勤労所得を定年時には同じに持っていく戦略と実行が必要です。

　企業も、理想的には、B/Sでの稼ぎを、営業利益とイコールにすることです。

　奇しくも、国際会計基準の利益は、包括利益＊です。

　儲けに色をつけないということです。

　業界の垣根がなくなりましたし、P/LでもB/Sでも、割り切って稼ぐこの気持ちが大切だと自分では思うんです。

＊包括利益

従来の当期純利益に、保有株式の 含み損益の変動額等を加えたものが包括利益。(ネットより)

salaried workers must have the same strategy and execution to take unearned and earned income at the time of retirement.

It is ideal for companies to make money in the B/S equal to operating income.

The profit of the International Accounting standard is a comprehensive income*.

There is no boundary in the industry. I think it is important to understand both P/L and B/S.

*Comprehensive Income (or earnings) is a specific term used in companies' financial reporting from the company-whole point of view. Because that use excludes the effects of changing ownership interest, an economic measure of comprehensive income is necessary for financial analysis from the shareholders' point of view. (from Wikipedia)

11. 本郷流投資の考え方
心乱（試行錯誤）の投資術（笑）

本郷流投資の考え方

　思い返せば、ずいぶん投資は失敗してきました。それでも最近はだいぶ改善されてマアマアの成績です。

　えらそうで恐縮ですが、本郷流投資の考え方を書いて見ます。

　私の投資術は次の通りです。でも、絶対ではありません。環境が変われば豹変します。

　私は、まず「自分でまずやって見ます」（だから失敗も多いのですが（笑））。

　その結果の投資術です。

11.
Under the Hongo Method
My investments of Trial and Error (laughs)

Under the Hongo Method

I've failed many times at investment. However, I have improved to a good level in recent times.

I would like to introduce you to the Hongo method.

My investment skills are as follows. However, they are not absolute. If the surrounding circumstances change, investment skills must also be changed accordingly.

I try everything by myself (That is why I make a lot of mistakes (laugh)).

The following showcases the results of my investment trials.

①人間とは愚か者と思って、投資機会に望むこと。

　決して、オレは投資の天才と思っていけません。

　ビギナーズラックかもしれません。

②投資は、資産価値に目をつけるのではなく、将来のキャッシュフローを生むかどうかで考える。

③投資を考える場合、やはり不動産投資は、長期的に投資の王様です。

④将来的には、不労所得と勤労所得を同じに持っていく努力が必要です。

　サラリーマンは退職時の自分の所得が、不労所得とイーブンになるのが理想です（なかなか（笑））。

⑤強欲は、敵だ！（素敵だ？）

　（欲は海水やで　飲めば飲むほど　のどが渇くもんや）

　常にいつでも、売却を考えるのが重要（これが難しいんだよ

①Try investment knowing that a man is a fool.

You do not think that I am an investment genius by any means.

You think you might have beginner's luck.

②Proper investment does not entail looking at the value of assets, but rather, is more about considering whether it will produce future cash flow.

③When thinking about investments, real estate investment is the king of investments for the long term.

④In the future, we need to put efforts to bring unearned income and income from working at the same level.

It is ideal for income received by salaried workers at the time of retirement to be equal to their unearned income.

⑤Greed is the enemy!

Greed is like the ocean–the more you drink it, the thirstier you become.

ね(笑))。

⑥絶対損してはダメ!
　努力して損する、こんなバカなことはない。

⑦だから、環境変化には敏感になれ。
　すべての投資資産を売ることも辞さない。
　下がったら、また買えばいい。

It is always important to think about selling your assets (This is difficult (laugh)).

⑥Never lose!

There is nothing like losing as a result of trying.

⑦Therefore, be sensitive to change in circumstances.

Do not be afraid to sell all of your investment assets if you need to.

You can repurchase them when their values go down in the future.

第2章

鳥の眼・虫の眼・魚の眼

その①

私の鳥の眼 マクロの眼

Chapter 2

Bird eye, insect eye, fish eye
①My bird eye, macro eyes

3つの眼

　よく言われることですが、投資を考える際には、「鳥の眼、虫の眼、魚の眼」の「3つの眼」が重要です。

　まず、1つ目の「鳥の眼」。鳥のように大空から俯瞰してみる広い視点が必要です。いわば、マクロの眼、長期的視点です。

　2つ目が「虫の眼」。虫のように地を這って、身近から詳細に視る眼も必要です。

　ミクロの眼です。実務にはこの嗅覚がとても大事で、投資のキモでもあります。

　でも、これだけでは不十分なんですね。

　さらに3つ目の「魚の眼」。これも不可欠です。魚は水中で絶えず危険な目にあいます。そして危険に対して瞬時に対応するため、俊敏な動きをします。

　投資環境が変わった場合に、すぐ環境の変化に対応できる魚のような俊敏さも不可欠です。ヤバイと思ったらすぐ損切り、撤退の勇気も必要です。

　余談ですが、魚のウロコを素材にした化粧品が開発されたことがあります。

　魚は岩に毎日ぶつかりますので、傷だらけです。でも、すぐ回復して肌がスベスベになります。これは、魚のウロコが回復

Three eyes

It is often said that we should think about investments using a bird's eye view.

The insect and fish viewpoints are also necessary.

At first, it is necessary to take a broad view from the sky like bird. This wide view is a long-term perspective.

In addition, it is necessary to crawl on the ground like an insect, and see things in detail. This is a close up view.

The sense of smell is also very important, and it is one of the most important characteristics for investment.

But this alone is not enough.

In addition, the fish's point of view is also indispensable. Fish are constantly swimming using their sharp eyes. They have great agility and are able to change their direction at any time.

剤の役割を果たすからだそうです。

この特性を使って、肌荒れ、シワ取りによく効くスキンクリームを作ったのです。

売れたかどうかは定かでありません（笑）。

私の鳥の眼

私は次の２つの理論を根拠として、投資判断を考えています。

これが、現在の私の鳥の眼です。

If the investment environment changes, agility, similar to a fish is essential. If you think the (financial) situation is bad, you need to cut your losses and withdraw at once.

As an aside, cosmetics have been developed from fish scales.

Because fish come into contact with rocks and stones every day, they easily become wounded. However, their skin soon recovers and becomes smooth again. This is because the fish scales aid recovery.

Using this characteristic, a pharmaceutical company made skin cream that works well for rough skin as well as removing wrinkles (I'm not sure if it is on sale or not!).

My bird eye

I think the following two theories are based on investment decisions.

This is my current bird's eye view.

第2章 鳥の眼・虫の眼・魚の眼 その①私の鳥の眼 マクロの眼

1. シムズ理論
最後はインフレ

今、シムズ理論*が話題となっています。

*シムズ理論とは、正確にいえば「物価の財政理論（the Fiscal Theory of Price Level）」、略して「FTPL」といわれるものです。2011年にノーベル経済学賞を受賞したクリストファー・シムズ（Christopher Albert Sims　Princeton University）米プリンストン大学教授が提唱。

シムズ理論とは

この理論は、次のような話です（私はちゃんと読んでいません。受け売りです）。
- 現在のような超低金利下では、金融政策（量的緩和）だけでは、物価はあがらない
- 物価上昇のためには、財政拡大が必要

Chapter 2 Bird eye, insect eye, fish eye ①My bird eye, macro eyes

1.
The Sims Theory
Ultimately, inflation

Now, The Sims Theory* has become topical.

*The "Sims theory" is "the Fiscal theory of Price level", which is called "FTPL" for short.

Christopher Albert Sims, (Princeton University), who won the Nobel Prize in Economics, submitted this theory in 2011.

What is The Sims theory?

I will explain this theory in the below story (I haven't read it properly).

Under such ultra-low interest rates, monetary policy (quantitative easing) does not raise prices.

- 減税も必要
- その結果、財政赤字が増え、国の借金が増えるが、その借金はインフレで実質チャラにする

日本政府の反応

　日本の政府もこの理論に大変興味があるといいます。深く考えなくても、とても、政府には都合のいい理屈です。
　大体、財政赤字を縮める努力が要りません（笑）。
　私は、政府はこの理論を取り入れるのではないかと思っています。
　すると、将来インフレになりますよね。

資産防衛が必要

　インフレになれば、私達の資産も目減りします。

If they want to raise prices, the government also needs to expand its fiscal policy.

Tax cuts are also necessary.

As a result, the budget deficit increases, the debt of the country increases, and the debt will write off any inflation.

Japanese Government Reaction

The Japanese Government is also very interested in this theory. Without thinking too deeply, it is a very "convenient logic" for the government.

They don't really need to make any real effort to decrease any deficits (laughs).

I think the government will adopt this theory, resulting in inflation in the future.

Asset Protection Required

When it comes to inflation, our assets will

ですから、インフレ対応の資産防衛策が必至です。

私の個人的意見ですが、資産防衛だけでは、目減りします。増やす努力も必要です。

適当なインフレレベル

適切なインフレレベルで金融緩和と財政政策がやめることができるのでしょうか？

シロート的な意見で恐縮ですが、一旦インフレに火がついたら、政策で止めることができるのでしょうか？

私は、無理だと思うのですね。とことんまで行くのではと思っています。

ハイパーインフレの心配する人がいますが、それは当分ないのではないでしょうか？

ハイパーインフレになるとすれば、1800兆円といわれる個人金融資産を使い切った時？

also be slashed.

Therefore, we have to protect our assets from inflation.

My personal opinion is that just asset protection is not enough. We must make more effort to increase our assets.

Moderate Inflation Level

Can monetary easing and fiscal policy be stopped at an appropriate inflation level?

I am sorry for my amateur opinion, but if inflation happens, the government may not be able to stop it.

By the way, there are people who are worried about hyperinflation, but it hasn't happened yet.

If hyperinflation does happen, Japan will spend money on personal financial assets of about 1,800 trillion yen.

第2章 鳥の眼・虫の眼・魚の眼 その①私の鳥の眼 マクロの眼

2.
トマ・ピケティ理論
資本収益率 (r) は経済成長率 (g) よりも常に大きい!

資本収益率 (r) は経済成長率 (g) よりも常に大きい!

この法則は、トマ・ピケティ (Thomas Piketty)*の『21世紀の資本』(みすず書房、2014年)*からの引用です。

ベストセラーになった有名な本です。

著者の分析によりますと、

「長期的にみると、資本収益率 (r) は経済成長率 (g) よりも常に大きく (r>g)、資産によって得られる富は、労働によって得られる富よりも大きい」*

その結果、

「富の集中が起こり、貧富の差が広がる」

とされています。

Chapter 2 Bird eye, insect eye, fish eye ①My bird eye, macro eyes

2.
Thomas Pikketty Theory
The capital return rate (R) is always greater than the economic growth rate (G)!

The capital return rate (R) is always greater than the economic growth rate (G)!

This is from the book, "21st Century Capital" by Thomas Piketty*.

This famous book became a bestseller.

According to the author's analysis,

"In the long term, the return on capital (R) is always greater than the economic growth rate (G). Wealth gained by assets is greater than the wealth gained by Labor"*.

As a result,

"The concentration of wealth is going to

＊トマ・ピケティ（Thomas Piketty,1971年〜）とは

　経済的不平等についての専門家であり、資本主義と格差拡大の関係について論証した「21世紀の資本」で一躍世界から注目を集めた。

＊長期的にみると、資本収益率（r）は経済成長率（g）よりも大きい。資本から得られる収益率が経済成長率を上回れば上回るほど、それだけ富は資本家へ蓄積される。そして、富が公平に分配されないことによって、貧困が社会や経済の不安定を引き起こすということを主題としている。

＊資本（ストック）が生み出す収益率が、資本収益率（ r ; return on capital）です。例えば、100万円の資本を使って、利息や投資などで1年間に5万円の収益を上げれば、資本収

widen the gap between the rich and poor".

* Thomas Piketty, (1971 ~)

Thomas Piketty is an expert on economic inequality, and has drawn attention from the world in the "21st Century Capital", which demonstrated the relationship between capitalism and inequality.

* In the long term, the return on capital (R) is greater than the economic growth rate (G). The higher the rate of return from the capital, the more it outweighs the economic growth, the more wealth is accumulated in the capitalist. And the subject of poverty to cause social and economic instability by not being distributed fairly.

* The return on capital is the revenue ratio produced by the capital (stock).

For example, if you use a capital of one

益率（r）は5％になります。

　歴史的に見た資本収益率（r）は、4〜5％です。（以上、ネットより）

「資産によって得られる富」

　私も昔から、なんとなく、そう思っていたのですが、なるほどなーと腹オチしましたね。
　難しく考えなくても、労働だけで小金持ちになった人は多数いますが、大金持ちになった人は、私の経験でも皆無ですものね。
　IPO長者、これだって、キャピタルゲインです。
　あのトランプだって、不動産王ですから、「資産によって得られる富」で大金持ちになりました。

million yen to increase the revenue of 50,000 yen per year for interest and investment, the return on capital (R) is 5%.

Historically, the capital rate of Return (R) is 4-5%. (from the Internet)

I Totally Agree With This

I used to think this way. Because of my past experience, this theory is very clear to me.

Even without thinking or trying too much, there are many people who have become a little wealthy through work (labor). However, in my experience, there are no people who have become super wealthy.

IPO millionaire-this is a capital gain.

Donald Trump is a real estate tycoon. He became a millionaire from "wealth gained by assets".

3. 私の見立て
2つの理論を踏まえて

長期的にはインフレ

　政府にとって都合のいい理論が出ましたね。シムズ理論は、行政にとても便利な理論です。

　だって、政府の負債は弁済しないで、インフレで返すのですから……。

　ですから、私は、将来インフレになると思っています。

　ただ悩ましいのは、全部インフレではないことです。インフレもあればデフレもあり？　かな。

　これだけ、技術のイノベーションが起これば、モノは供給不足になりません。

　生産力が飛躍的に向上していますものね。世界大戦でも起これば別ですが。

Chapter 2 Bird eye, insect eye, fish eye ①My bird eye, macro eyes

3.
My opinion
Based on the two theories

Inflation in The Long Run

The Sims theory is a very useful theory for the Government.

This is because the government's debt is not repaid. The debt is returned through inflation.

Therefore, I think inflation will come in the future.

One annoying point is that all assets and products are not affected by inflation or deflation.

If innovation in technology develops more, there will never be any supply problems– there will be no shortages.

低金利は続く*

Cash is King to cash is stone.
(お金は無価値のだだの石ころに戻った)(水野和夫氏「マイナス金利 黒田バズーカは誤爆した」『文藝春秋』2016年4月号、文藝春秋)

20年に渡っての低金利です。

これから、この低金利は続くのでしょうか?

今、1億円定期にしても、利息は1年で1万円。

アーア(笑)。

でも、日本は、投資機会が少ないから、この低金利は続くのではないでしょうか? もしかして"永遠のゼロ"(平山賢一氏)?

なにより、国債を大量発行している、政府が金利上昇は困ります。

ですから、適度な借り入れ経営(レバレッジ)は、必要でしょうね。

Over the years, production has improved dramatically. If there is a world wide war, there will be many shortages. Supply chains will be broken, and inflation will be triggered.

Low Interest Rates Continue *

Cash is to king as cash is to stone (Mr. Kazuo Mizuno) . Money is worthless. Its value is the same as a pebble.

Low interest rates have continued for 20 years.

Will low interest rate continue?

If we deposit 100 million yen for one year in a bank, we can only make 10,000 yen.

 Ah! (Laughs)

But in Japan, since there are few opportunities for investment, will this low interest rate continue? "Eternal zero(Mr. Kenichi Hirayama)" -forever a zero rate!?

Above all, a government that is issuing

オレは、無借金経営だ！と威張ってもいられない時代かな？

＊「七二の法則」（七二を金利で割ると、複利で元金が倍になるまでの年数が大雑把にわかるという法則）があります。

これで計算しますと、現在の日本の預金金利（0.01％）では元金を倍にするのに約7200年もかかります。（『マイナス金利でも年12％稼ぐ黄金のノウハウ』浅井 隆著、第二海援隊、2016年）

large amounts of government bonds will be troubled by rising interest rates.

Therefore, management using leverage is necessary.

By the way, "My company doesn't have any debt". Many business leaders often proudly say this. However I think it's not a good policy.

* "72 's Law"

(A rule of thumb is that if you divide 72 by interest rates, you can see roughly how many years the principal is doubled by compounding interest)

In this calculation, the current Japanese deposit rate (0.01%) takes about 7200 years to double the principal. ("The golden know-how to earn 12% of negative interest rate" by Takashi Asai)

年利7％

30年前には大体年利7％を前提として、10年で倍になるシナリオの資産運用の本を私は書いた記憶があります。

隔世の感があります。

資産インフレ

低金利でインフレ、すると、資産インフレですよね。

ですから、積極的に投資機会を探す、これが、資産防衛であり、資産創造ではないでしょうか？

Annual Interest rate 7%

30 years ago, I remember writing a book on asset management for a scenario that doubles in 10 years, assuming a roughly 7% annual interest rate.

However this interest rate is gone.

Asset Inflation

Low interest rates continue, but some assets will rise in the future. This is a kind of asset inflation.

You should be actively looking for investment opportunities. Finding properties which will increase in value in the future are rare. This is not only protection for your assets but also asset acquisition.

そして、トマ・ピケティ

なんといっても、資本収益率（r）＞経済成長率（g）です。

財務の稼ぎが、労働の稼ぎを上回る、積極的に資産所得をとりにいく所以です。

すると私の見立てでは、長期的には、「インフレ対応の資産形成、そして、財務の稼ぎを増やす」、こうなります。

Thomas Piketty

The capital return rate (R) > Economic growth rate (G).

This theory is a reason for investing in assets.

So, in my estimation, in the long run, we should invest in assets that are suited to future inflation and will provide us with (big) financial returns.

第3章

鳥の眼・虫の眼・魚の眼

その②

私の虫の眼 実践の眼

Chapter 3

Bird eye, insect eye, fish eye
②My insect eye, micro eyes

宝くじも買わなきゃ当たらない

Knowing－Doing Gap.

知ることとやることのギャップ。これが実に大きい。

いいなと思って興味を持つのですが、なぜかやらない。これは、人間の性なんでしょうね。

あるいは、過去に手痛くやられたトラウマでできない。これらのバリアを超えて、ファイナンスに一歩踏み出す。

これって実に大変なことなんですね。

でも、「宝くじも買わなきゃ当たらない」

私は、いつもこう思っています。

私の実践

能書きを言う前に私の実践を書きます。

書きながら思ったのですが、なんと投資ポリシーのないこと（笑）。

"If you never buy a lottery ticket, you'll never win the lottery"

"The gap between knowing and doing things".

The gap between knowing and doing things is very big.

We usually recognize this, but we don't follow it. This is human nature, isn't it?

Bad investment experiences from our past (trauma) may hold us back. Let's forget those bad memories, and move on.

Let's go! (laughs)

Repeat-we must buy a lottery ticket to have a chance of winning.

My Practice

Let's talk about my investment experience.

I have a "no thinking investment policy" (dabohaze).

ダボハゼだね。

恥ずかしながら、私の最近の投資を紹介します。

I'm embarrassed to talk about my recent investments.

第3章　鳥の眼・虫の眼・魚の眼　その②私の虫の眼　実践の眼

1.

一通貨二金利
同じ通貨でも国によって金利が違う

カンボジアへの投資

　たまたま、数年前にカンボジア、プノンペンに弊社の現地法人を作りました。その時、カンボジアは米ドルが自由に使える国だとわかりました。

　米ドル預金ができ、なおかつ金利も高い（図1参照）。

　米国本土の金利が低金利ですが、カンボジアの米ドル預金は高い。

　一通貨二金利ということがあるんですね。

　そこで、この高金利を利用して、定期預金をして、現地の経費の足しにしようと、考えました。

　事業が軌道に乗るまで時間がかかるので、その前に金利で赤字を補填するスキームです。

Chapter 3 Bird eye, insect eye, fish eye ②My insect eye, micro eyes

1.
US dollar has two different interest rates though the same currency

Investing in Cambodia

By chance, I opened our local subsidiary in Phnom Penh, Cambodia, 7 years ago. At that time, I realized that in Cambodia US currency can be freely used.

US dollar interest rates are high (See Figure 1).

In mainland US interest rates are low, but US deposit rates are high in Cambodia.

In other words, one currency has two interest rates.

When I knew this, I decided to use this

これは、うまく行きましたね。

定期の金利で現地スタッフの給与が払えたし、なにより、為替で儲かりました。

80円で送金していましたから、その後の円安で利益が取れました。

余談ですが、ソフトバンクがスプリントへ投資した時も、1ドル80円でした。もう円高はお仕舞いだと決断して、投資したという話を雑誌で読みました。

私の場合は、為替を考えない投資でして、単なる運で儲かっただけです。

エライ違いです。

海外進出は、金利との合わせ技

特に新興国への投資は、金利が高いので金利との組み合わ

high interest rate. And I made deposits to compensate for local staff's expenses.

It went well.

I was able to pay the local staff welland in addition, still make a profit because of the exchange rate.

As an aside, when SoftBank invested in Sprint, the exchange rate was 80 yen per 1US dollar. I read in a magazine that Mr. Son (SoftBank CEO) thought the yen rate had already peaked, so he decided to invest.

However, in my case, I didn't think about the future of the yen. I made profit by luck– it's a huge difference!

It is necessary to combine technique with interest rates when expanding into overseas expansion operations

I highly recommend this if you are investing

せがお薦めです。

　金利で進出する現地法人の経費の足しにする。軌道に乗るまでの赤字の補填で、預金をしておく。

　為替のリスクはもちろんありますが、どうせ進出したんだから、長期にほって置けばいいと私は思っています。

図1　カンボジアある日系現地銀行の金利水準

定期預金			
通貨	米ドル	クメールリエル	タイバーツ
1ヶ月	3.50%	4.00%	3.50%
2ヶ月	3.75%	4.25%	3.75%
3ヶ月	4.00%	5.00%	4.00%
6ヶ月	4.50%	5.50%	4.50%
9ヶ月	5.50%	6.50%	5.50%
12ヶ月	6.50%	7.50%	6.50%
24ヶ月	7.00%	8.00%	7.00%
36ヶ月	7.00%	8.00%	7.00%

2017年6月現在

in emerging markets because of the high interest rates.

The money made on interest will compensate for the expense of the subsidiary. We can use the high interest rate to compensate for any initial losses until we turn a profit.

Of course there is a risk when investing in foreign exchanges. When expanding our overseas operations, we have to leave money in that country for a long period of time. Because of this there is little lisk.

Figure 1   Interest rate of Japanese local bank in Cambodia

Time deposit			
currency	**US dollar**	**Khmer Riel**	**Thai Baht**
1 month	3.50%	4.00%	3.50%
2months	3.75%	4.25%	3.75%
3months	4.00%	5.00%	4.00%
6months	4.50%	5.50%	4.50%
9months	5.50%	6.50%	5.50%
12months	6.50%	7.50%	6.50%
24months	7.00%	8.00%	7.00%
36months	7.00%	8.00%	7.00%

As of June 2017

円ドル勝負

これは、私は良くやりました。

ボラティリティ(volatility)＊が短期で起こります。

図２を見て下さい。

今までは、ボラティリティは、比較的長期に起こりました。

でも、今は、１年で平気で２割は価格が動きます。ということは、短期勝負ができます。

＊ボラティリティ(volatility)とは、広義には資産価格の変動の激しさを表すパラメータ。(ネットより)

為替の投資は相手国で高利運用ができる国が良い

私は、米ドルに変えて、もし円高になって損をしたら、わりきって米ドルで運用します。

I often invest in US dollars and convert to Japanese Yen

The exchange rate can be volatile* so it is a good opportunity to invest (See Figure 2).

Last year, there was a 20% shift in the exchange rate.

These days, we can play the short-term game.

* Volatility is a parameter that represents the intensity of fluctuations in asset prices in a broad sense. (from the Internet)

Foreign exchange investment is suitable for a country where other countries can operate at high yields easily

I will change my money to US dollars, and if I lose yen, I will continue to operate in US

米国は、高利回りの商品が手に入ります。

例えば、ドル建ての金利の高い、例えば、劣後債＊を買って待ちます。

今保有しているのは、ロシアのルーブル債（年利11％）とドイツ銀行（年6％）の劣後債です。

円高になりましたら、また、円に交換します。

これは、比較的パフォーマンスがいいですね。

ポイントは、日本の金利が低いのでできるんですね。円キャリーと同じです。

＊劣後債

企業が社債を発行する際、通常無担保で発行される社債を一般無担保社債もしくは優先社債（シニア債）というが、一般無担保社債と比べて、元本および利息の支払い順位の低い社債を劣後債ないし劣後社債（またはシニア債に対しジュニア債）

dollars.

In the United States it is possible to get many high yield products.

For example, I had a high interest rate of dollar denominated, subordinated bonds*.

I now have the Russian ruble bond (annual rate of 11%) and German Bank (6%) subordinated bond.

When the yen becomes strong, we can exchange the currency back to yen.

We can make a relatively good profit doing this.

The point is, Japanese interest rates are low-the same as "Yen carry".

* Subordinated bonds

When companies issue corporate bonds, generally, unsecured bonds or preferred corporate bonds (senior bonds), which are issued in unsecured terms, are referred to as lower bonds or subordinated bonds (or

と呼ぶ。債務不履行のリスクが大きい分、利回りは相対的に高く設定されている。(ネットより)

図2　円ドル為替の推移

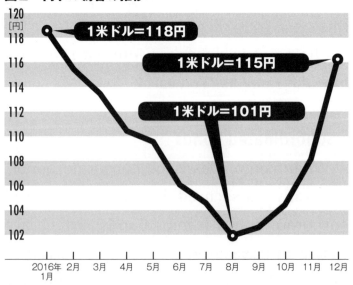

※月間の平均レート

junior bonds to senior bonds) as compared to general unsecured bonds. The greater the risk of default, the higher the yield is set. (from the Internet)

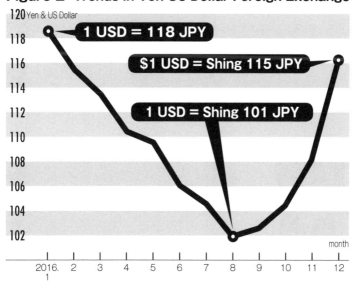

Figure 2 Trends in Yen US Dollar Foreign Exchange

※Average monthly rate

2.
短期の延長が長期!
長期の中の短期ではない

　虫の眼は、長期と短期の両方を持っていなければなりません。

　雑駁に言います。

2.
A long-term investment is not necessary

We should focus on the volatile situation happening now, and adjust accordingly.

The eye of the insect must have both a long term and a short term view. This is common sense in the investment world. Therefore, we can usually distinguish a long term and a short term investment.

But not now.

If you make short-term investments repeatedly, they will become the long-term investments.

長期的視点

①リスクオフ……安定性

②キャッシュフロー

③ストック

短期的視点

①リスクオン……やや投機性

②キャピタルゲイン

③フロー

　でも、理屈はそうですが、前述したように、ボラティリティが短期で起こります。

　長期投資で始めても、短期勝負の場面がすぐ起きます。

　ですから、私は、短期の延長として長期を捉えるのがいいのではと思っています。

Long-term perspective

Risk off......Stability*
Cash Flow

*Stability

We should have properties which produce cash flow in the long term.

Short-term perspective

Risk on......Somewhat speculative*
Capital Gains
High performance

But the theory is, as I mentioned earlier, that volatility happens in the short term.

Even if you start with long-term investments, you will soon get a short-term gain.

Therefore, I think we should focus on current situation.

*In the short term there is risk and little stability. Any capital gains are only temporary but we can have a good performance.

Chapter 3　Bird eye, insect eye, fish eye　②My insect eye, micro eyes

3.
定期預金より銀行株
金利よりも配当

短期のボラティリティ

　短期の大きなボラティリティは、株式でも勝負ができます（図3）。

　前述しましたが、1億円の定期預金の利息は1年で1万円です。

　すると、配当が良い銀行株は、預金よりうまみがあります。

　マイナス金利で銀行株が下がった時に、配当目的で銀行株を買った人が知り合いでいます。

　単純な話、銀行から借金をして銀行株を買う、これも儲け方ですよね。

Chapter 3 Bird eye, insect eye, fish eye ②My insect eye, micro eyes

3.
Bank stock is much better than bank deposits
Dividends are much higher than interest rates

If you deposit money into a bank, you can buy the bank's shares

In the short term, during high volatility, we have the opportunity to buy stock (See Figure 3).

Bank stocks that have high dividends are more profitable than deposits.

When the bank shares go down with a negative interest rate, there are people who buy the bank stock for dividend purposes.

Borrowing money from a bank and buying

買うタイミングの失敗

「銀行預金するなら、銀行株を買う」

そこで、「配当が良い銀行株」を探したら、上位にあおぞら銀行が出てきました。

とりあえず、買ってみたら、そのあと暴落です。

株価の予測と買うタイミングは重要です(利は元にあります)。

それと配当利回りが過去の実績です。当たり前ですが、来期の予想ではありません。

今、配当利回りランキングを見ると、株価が下がった分、利回りが上がっています。

(追記　最近あおぞら銀行の株価を見ましたら、買った値段より上がっていましたので売却しました。配当落ちのあとですから、配当も確保できました。)

a bank (through shares), is also a good way of making a profit.

Failure

When I searched for "bank stocks with good dividends", the Aozora bank came out on top.

Unfortunately, after I purchased Aozora Bank stock, their stock dropped.

The forecast of the stock price and timing are important (the profit depends on purchase price).

Listed dividend yields (dividend yield rankings) are not current.

This is no forecast for the next fiscal year.

(I noticed the stock price of Aozora bank has risen, so I sold my stock to make a profit. I was able to secure dividends after the dividends fell.)

図3　日経平均株価の推移

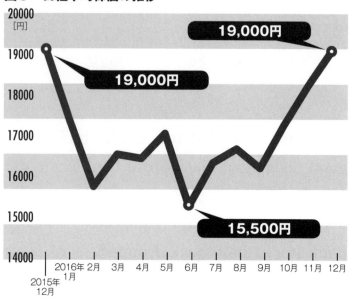

Figure 3 Changes in Nikkei Stock Average

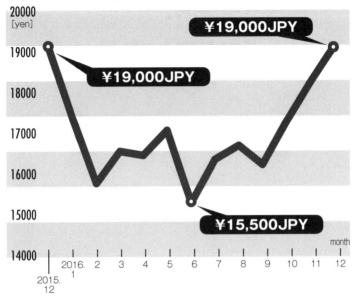

4.
利は元にあり
安く仕入れる

買うタイミング

資産の購入も、利は元にありです。

買うタイミングが一番重要です。

金融(ファイナンス)を、値づけと喝破した人がいます。蓋し、卓見です。

一般に、株でも不動産でも、高くなってから買うんですね。

うまいへたではなく、これは経済学というより心理学です。

理想的には、逆張りですが、なかなかねー(笑)。

4.
Profit depends on purchase price

Good timing is important when you buy assets

Investment profit depends on purchase price.

The best time to buy is the most important.

Someone said that finance means "buying price". I agree!

In general, even with stock and real estate, we tend to buy it at higher prices.

It is not a good thing, but this is psychology rather than economics.

M&Aも仕入れがキモ

M&Aも買収会社のキャッシュフローを買うわけですから、仕入れがキモです。

安く買うことができれば、利回りがグンとあがります。

投資は不景気な時こそチャンス

不況の時は、業績不振の事業を安く買えますから、積極的な経営者にとってはまたとないチャンスでした。昔は「できる経営者は、不況期に設備投資をする」という格言がありました。

投資もつくづく「利は元にあり」です。

The purchase of M&A also depends on purchase price

M&A buys the cash flow of the acquisition company.

If you buy it at a low price, the yields will go up.

A recession is a good opportunity to buy assets

The recession was a chance for aggressive managers to buy low-performing businesses. In the past, there was a saying that "smart business leaders invest in capital during the recession period".

Investment also depends on purchase price.

第3章　鳥の眼・虫の眼・魚の眼　その②私の虫の眼　実践の眼

5.
100％のパフォーマンスを求めない
名人、天井売らず底買わず！

ポンド買いの失敗

　イギリスのEU離脱（Brexit）に賭けて、ポンド買いをしました。これは見事失敗でした。

　売り時を間違えたんですね。

　投票が始まる前は、EU離脱はないとの憶測で、ポンドが上がりましたね。

Chapter 3 Bird eye, insect eye, fish eye ②My insect eye, micro eyes

5.
Don't ask for 100% performance

Super Investment Specialist :
"Do not buy at the lowest price,
and sell before it reaches the the ceiling!"

Failure to buy pounds

I bet on the British EU withdrawal (Brexit) and bought pounds. But I completely failed.

It was the wrong time to sell.

Before the voting began, the pound went up with speculation that there would be no EU withdrawal.

図4　Brexitとポンド円の為替レート

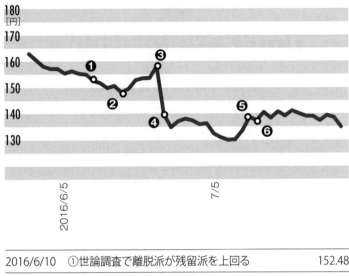

2016/6/10	①世論調査で離脱派が残留派を上回る	152.48
2016/6/16	②残留派の議員が銃殺される	148.56
2016/6/23	③国民投票	157.90
2016/6/24	④投票の結果、離脱が過半数。キャメロン首相辞意を表明	139.78
2016/7/12	⑤メイが保守党党首に	138.63
2016/7/13	⑥メイ首相就任	137.34

Figure 4 Brexit and Pound Sterling Exchange Rates

2016/6/10	① Opinion survey surpasses remnants in opinion poll	152.48
2016/6/16	② Legislative members of the residents are shot dead	148.56
2016/6/23	③ Referendum	157.90
2016/6/24	④ As a result of voting, withdrawal is a majority. Prime Minister Cameron announced his resignation	139.78
2016/7/12	⑤ May is the president of the Conservative Party	138.63
2016/7/13	⑥ Inauguration of Prime Minister May	137.34

「売ろう」と思ったんです。

　ところが欲を出したんですね。もっと上がると思ったんです。

　その後、情勢が残留派に不利になり、損をしました。

　「腹八分」日本語にはとてもいい言葉があります（笑）。

　つくづく、上記の名人には程遠い！

　その後、専門家に聞きましたら、為替は、先行で動くといいます。

　ですから、Brexitの投票が始まる前が一番高いんですね。

　勉強になりました。

I thought, "sell".

However, I was greedy. I thought it would go up more.

Eventually, the Brexit situation worsened and I lost money.

There is a very good Japanese word "belly eight" (hara-hatibu) (laughs).

I am still not an export.

After that, I asked an expert about Brexit. The exchange rate was expected to rise.

It was the highest just before the Brexit vote.

I was studying this situation.

6.

休日でも稼げる商売
太陽光投資

不動産は上がりすぎ？

「休日でも稼げる商売」

私が数十年にわたって好きな言葉です。

まず、不動産投資。長期的には、投資の王様です。

資産インフレの目安も不動産ですね。

何回か出した拙著*でも触れていますが、「定年時の年収＝家賃収入」が理想です。

でも、今の時点（2017年6月時点）では、不動産投資は高くなりすぎて、私的には買う気にはならないのですね。

都心の一等地で利回り2％です。

自己資金ででも買わないと、危険だなーと思ってしまいます（低金利が続くなら、2％でも買いということになるのですが

Chapter 3 Bird eye, insect eye, fish eye ②My insect eye, micro eyes

6.
A business to make money even when on holiday
Solar Investment

Is this real estate gone too far?

"A business to make money even when on holiday"

That's a phrase I've liked over the decades.

Real estate investment is king.

In the long run, real estate will surely be affected by inflation.

Even in my book*, which has been printed several times, "Income at the time of retirement = Rent".

But as of June 2017, real estate investment was too high,so I don't plan to buy it.

……。でもね)。

＊『金持ちの脳みそ』(実業之日本社、2003年)、『お金は貯める前に使いなさい!』(成美文庫、2012年)

空き家リスクなし

「太陽光投資」

　私的におもしろいと思っているのが、太陽光投資です。

　今、これに凝っています。私の投資の主力をこれにおいています。

　これも、小口化して販売されています。

　太陽光には、電力会社の固定買取制度(FIT)が20年あります。

　つまり、20年固定収入が入ります。

Yields are only 2% in prime city center locations.

I think it is dangerous if I use my own money to buy real estate (If low interest rates continue, you will be able to buy real estate, but I think it's dangerous).

*"Rich Brains" (Jitsugyo-no-nihon, 2003),"Use it before you earn money!" (Narumi Bunko, 2012)

No empty risk

"Solar Investment"

As a private investment, I think solar power is interesting.

Now I'm hooked on this. This is the mainstay of my investment.

Solar packages are also sold in small amounts.

In solar investment, the power company's

不動産会社の社長が太陽光投資をしてつくづく言ってました。

「不動産は空き家リスクがあるけど、太陽光は、空き家リスクがない」

　蓋し、名言です。

すべてを動産と考える
流動化の時代の三種の神器

　私は、不動産*というのが近い将来なくなるのでは？ と思っています。

　すべて、流動化、動産化すると思っています。

　私は、勝手に流動化の三種の神器を次のように決めています。

「キャッシュフロー、レバレッジ、流動化（liquidation）」

　これを根拠に長期投資を考えます。

fixed purchase system (FIT) continues for 20 years.

20 years of fixed income!

The president of a real estate company who invested in solar power said,

"Real estate has an empty risk, whereas solar investment does not"

It's probably a smart statement.

The age of liquidation:Think of everything as a chattel! There are three kinds of sacred treasures (sansyu-no-jingi)

I think real estate* will change.

All properties will become chattels* that can be liquidized.

I have decided that the three kinds of sacred treasures of liquidation are as follows.

"Cash flow, leverage and liquidation"

Based on this, we can consider long-term

①キャッシュフロー

　何回も書きますが、値上がり期待だけでは投資をしません。

②レバレッジ*

　借金のトラウマがあるのですが、やっと私なりに払拭できました。

　それでも、フルローンは私的には怖いですね。

　ですから、50％ぐらいにレバは押さえています（最近は、70％ぐらいに上げています）。

③そして、流動化できるか？

　不動産リート*を待つまでもなく、なんでも、流動化の時代です。

　将来小口化して再販できるか、これもポイントです。

　私は、奥さん以外はすべて流動化する時代が来ると思っています。

investments.

①Cash Flow

I have written this many times, "I don't invest with the expectation of raising prices".

②Leverage*

I had a bad experience and memory (trauma) about debt I incurred in the past, but I was finally able to dispel it.

But still, taking out a full loan (100%) is quite scary–privately speaking.

50% leverage is ideal (Recently I've decided that 70% is even better) .

③Every asset can be liquidized, the same as Estate REIT*

Let's think about your assets.

If you buy an asset, can it be liquidated in the future? If the assets are liquidated, they can be resold easily. This is a key point.

I believe that there will be a time when everything will be liquidated.

＊不動産

　土地やそれに定着する建物・立ち木など。物のうち容易にその所在を変えることができないもの。

動産

　不動産以外のすべての財産。現金・商品など。(以上、ネットより)

＊無借金は正しい戦略か？

　低金利、将来のインフレを考えると、やはり、無借金経営は堅いですが、伸びしろがないのでは？と個人的には思います。

　M&Aを見ても、レバレッジは投資だけでなく、企業の成長戦略の一つです。

　あとは程度ですよね(笑)。

　銀行が一斉に回収に入った時は、過度のレバレッジは怖い。

＊REIT (リート) とは、Real Estate Investment Trust (不動産投資信託) の略称で、投資家から資金を集めて不動産を運用して得た賃料収入等を元に投資家に分配する金融商品です。 米国で1960年代に誕生し、1990年代に急速に拡大しました。

*Real Estate

Buildings and trees that are rooted to the land and it. The thing which cannot easily change the whereabouts of the thing.

*Chattel

All property except real estate. (Internet definition)

* Debt. Is it the right strategy?

Many Japanese companies hate being debt.

However, if we consider low interest rates and future inflation, moderate leveraging for our business is necessary, I think.

Even looking at M&A, leveraging is one of the investment strategies for corporate growth.

Excessive leverage is scary when the bank want to recover it's money.

* REIT is a financial instrument that distributes funds from investors; including real estate investment trusts to the investor based on the rental income earned from

不動産リートの注意点

　短期間ですが不動産リートにトライしました。アメリカの不動産リートです。

　雑誌で、褒めていたので、買ってみました。すごく便利な商品で、毎月分配してくれます。

「年金生活者向けの商品だ」との説明を受けました。

　でも、注意点は、毎月、元本と金利を一緒に分配します。

　ですから、毎月投資元本に「値上がり益がなければ」、減っていきます。

　私も誤解して、すごい配当だなと思っていたのですが、蛸足配当なんですね。

　私の場合、為替がうまくぶれて儲かりましたが、その時点ですぐ店じまいしました。

the investment house. REIT was born in the 1960s in United States and rapidly expanded in the 1990s.

Precautions for Real Estate REIT

I invested in real estate REIT(American Real Estate) for a short period of time.

I read in a magazine that it was a good performance, so I bought it. It was a very convenient product, and was distributed every month.

It was explained as, "A commodity for the pensioner".

But the caveat is that the share is both the principal as well as the interest rate each month.

So, every month, the principal investment will decrease .

I thought it was a great dividend, but I was mistaken.

In my case, the exchange was profitable, and I was able to close my investment.

第4章

鳥の眼・虫の眼・魚の眼

その③

私の魚の眼 流れを読む眼

Chapter 4

Bird eye, insect eye, fish eye
③My fish eye, the eye for of reading change in flow

第4章 鳥の眼・虫の眼・魚の眼　その③私の魚の眼　流れを読む眼

1.
第2のリーマンショックが来るか?
銀行から政府へ

第2のリーマンショックは来るのか?

　2、3年前から私の関心は、第2のリーマンショックが来るのだろうか? でした。

　私の魚の眼の中心が、今でもそれです。

　リーマンショックは2008年ですから、そろそろだなーというだけの話で根拠があるわけではありません(笑)。

　リーマン時との違いは、主役が銀行だったのが今は政府です。

　銀行は経営危機になれば、倒産か資金回収に回ります。そうすると、お金がギュッとしまります。

　でも、政府は　経営危機になれば、お札が刷れます。

　これは、大きな違いです。

Chapter 4 Bird eye, insect eye, fish eye ③My fish eye, the eye for of reading change in flow

1.
Is the second Lehman shock coming?

Is the second Lehman shock coming?

The Lehman shock was in 2008. I feel there will be another shock in the near future.

I'm concerned about this.

Therefore, if I make investments, I'm always thinking about the possibility of the next shock. But it's just my opinion and has no basis.

On the other hand, I have a completely different opinion. There is a big difference between the Lehman shock and today's economic situation. In 2008, the main

ですから、お金が不足することはないのかなー。第2のリーマンショックは、起こらない気もするんです。

正直わかりません。

そのため、起こっても驚かないようなリスク管理は必要だと自分では思っています。

character was the bank, but now it is the government.

If a bank falls into a crisis situation, it will go bankrupt or loans will be collected. Then money becomes hard to get.

But if there is a crisis in the government, more money will be printed. The Government will never go bankrupt.

This is a huge difference.

Therefore, with this line of thinking, the second Lehman shock should not happen (But I honestly don't know).

So, it's a good idea to manage risk in a way that we can cover every situation.

第4章 鳥の眼・虫の眼・魚の眼 その③私の魚の眼 流れを読む眼

2.
不動産投資
民泊解禁

不動産投資終わりの始まり

2018年1月から民泊*が解禁となります。

私の魚の眼は、来年の1月がターニングポイントではないかな?

こう思っています。

民泊が解禁されますと、皆インバウンドを想定していますが、国内の利用者も必ず増えます。高いホテルに泊まる層もありますが、安価でサービスの良い民泊も需要が増えます。

大航海時代(拙著『本郷孔洋の経営ノート2017』)が到来しますので、大旅行時代がきます。

すると、民泊用の不動産投資が始まります。

私の身近な例でも、貸室を民泊に切り替えたら家賃が2倍に取れます。

2.
Real estate investment

Real estate investment will be at turning point from 2018

Guest houses (Minpaku) will be allowed to operate from January ,2018.

I think the real estate industry will be booming.

Many tourists from overseas will stay in them.

Both inbound and outbound

I believe not only overseas tourists, but also a lot of domestic tourists will stay in them. There are some tiers of high-priced

今は法律上グレーですから、コソコソやらなければなりませんが、法律解禁になれば、堂々とできます。
　すると、利回りが上がります。
　不動産投資ブームが来るのでは、と密かに期待しています。
　来年ということは、今年から準備しても早くはありません。
　私も興味がありますので、情報を取っているところです。

hotels, but the demand for Guest houses with good service is increasing.

The New Great Voyage Period (my book "Management Note 2017") will come.

This means there will be an age of travel.

Real estate investment in Minpaku will quickly begin.

If you switch your existing real estate to Guest houses, you can at least double your rent (This is my experience).

Guest houses are in a legal gray zone now, but if they becomes legal, the image of guest houses will improve.

The yield will increase.

I secretly expect a real estate boom soon.

It's never too early to prepare, so I'm gathering information and researching about this.

首都圏の貸しビルの将来

ものすごい勢いで、都心部の不動産開発が行われています。でもどうでしょう？この勢いで、テナントがつくのでしょうか？私は、近い将来空室だらけになるのでは？と懸念しています。古いビルは、テナントがつかなくて困る時代が来るのでは？

需要は３割減

　シェアーオフィス、フリーアドレス、シェアーハウスが増えています。

　私の勝手な予想ですが、フリーアドレスにしただけで、借りる面積が３割少なくなります（実は弊社でも実践していました。引っ越しを期にフリーアドレスにしたところ、900坪借りていた面積が700坪で済みました）。

　ですから、古いビルから余って行くのではないかと思っています。

The future of the Metropolitan Lending Building

Real estate development in the inner city has taken off with great momentum.

If this momentum continues into the future, will there be enough tenants?

I think older buildings will become vacant in the near future.

Demand decreased by 30%

Shared offices, free addresses and share houses are becoming more popular.

It is my selfish expectation, if many tenants want to live in a shared environment, the shared area will decrease by about 30% compared to the more fixed areas previously used. Our office moved into a new building last year. I decided to make a free address

すると、再活用の時代が来る!

　余ったビルの再利用、これはすごいビジネスチャンスだと思っています。

　考えて見ますと、従来の不動産は、あまり頭を使いませんでした。

　それでも、需要があったんで、そんな必要がなかった。でも、これからは、不動産にも知恵が必要な時代です。

　でも、個人的には、おもしろい時代が始まると思っています。

　知恵次第で利回りが違う時代に突入する?

(not fix desk). Previously we were renting a space of 900 tsubo. Now we are renting a space of 700 tsubo. Our rental space has decreased by almost 30%.

Therefore, office demand will decrease in the near future. With this decrease in needed space, old buildings will become vacant.

The re-use age!

Real estate business has developed since World War 2. This is because the (Japanese) population increased.

Conventional real estate owners didn't think about this clearly.

Now we have to think about the real estate business seriously. How we can raise rental fees? This is a great business opportunity to reuse surplus buildings.

Personally, I think it's an interesting time to start.

魚の眼の目玉は不動産投資

すると、不動産の投資が王様になると、私は考えています。

＊住宅宿泊事業法（以下、民泊新法）は、民泊に関わる一連の事業者の適正な運営を確保しつつ、国内外からの宿泊需要に的確に対応し、観光客の来訪や滞在を促進することで日本経済の発展に寄与することを目指して定められる法律となります。民泊新法の対象となるのは、下記3種類の事業者となります。

①住宅宿泊事業者：民泊ホスト

②住宅宿泊管理業者：民泊運営代行会社

③住宅宿泊仲介業者：Airbnbをはじめとする民泊仲介サイト

民泊新法においては、①～③それぞれの事業者に対して「届出」や「登録」など事業運営において必要となる手続き、および事業者として実施するべき「業務」の内容、そして行政職員によるそれらの「監督」権限について詳しく定められ、違反時の罰

Depending on how we think (strategy), yields will differ.

My fish eye focus on real estate investment

I think that investment in real estate will become king again in the future.

* Housing Business Act (Minpaku new law) while ensuring the proper operation of a series of business operators involved in the Minpaku, it is a law that aims to contribute to the development of the Japan economy by responding adequately to the accommodation demand from the domestic and overseas and promoting the visitor's visit and stay. The following three types of businesses are eligible for the Minpaku new law.
①**Housing operator:** Minpaku host
②**Housing Accommodation Management:**

則についても厳しく規定されています。(以上、ネットより)

Minpaku Management Agency

③**Housing Brokerage:** Airbnb and other Minpaku brokerage sites

In the Minpaku new law, the procedures required for business operations such as "notification" and "registration" for Shing-Shing each business person as well as the contents of "business" to be implemented as a business operator, and those "supervisory" authority by administrative staff are provided in detail, and the penalties for violations are strictly regulated. (from the Internet)

【参考文献】(順不同)

『財テク社長学入門 オーナー社長のうまみを最大限発揮してどこが悪い!』本郷孔洋、山田淳一郎 著、大成出版社、1989年10月

「日本経済新聞」2017年4月7日

『金持ち父さん貧乏父さん アメリカの金持ちが教えてくれるお金の哲学』ロバート・キヨサキ、シャロン・レクター 著、白根美保子 訳、筑摩書房、2000年11月

『あれか、これか－「本当の値打ち」を見抜くファイナンス理論入門』野口真人 著、ダイヤモンド社、2016年4月

『21世紀の資本』トマ・ピケティ 著、山形浩生、守岡 桜、森本正史 訳、みすず書房、2014年12月

「マイナス金利 黒田バズーカは誤爆した」水野和夫 著(『文藝春秋』2016年4月号、文藝春秋)

『マイナス金利でも年12%稼ぐ黄金のノウハウ』浅井 隆 著、第二海援隊、2016年8月

『金持ちの脳みそ』拙著、実業之日本社、2003年9月

『お金はためる前に使いなさい!』拙著、成美文庫、2012年10月

『本郷孔洋の経営ノート2017 大航海時代のビジネスチャンス』拙著、東峰書房、2017年3月

(敬省略)

本書の英文は、Microsoftの翻訳サービス「Microsoft Translator」を参考として使用しています。

〈著者プロフィール〉

本郷 孔洋 (ほんごうよしひろ)
公認会計士・税理士

　辻・本郷グループ会長。辻・本郷 税理士法人前理事長。

　早稲田大学第一政経学部卒業、同大学大学院商学研究科修士課程修了。公認会計士登録。

　辻・本郷 税理士法人を設立し、理事長として総勢1400名のスタッフ、顧問先10000社の国内最大規模を誇る税理士法人へと育て上げる。会計の専門家として会計税務に携わって30余年、各界の経営者・起業家・著名人との交流を持つ。2016年1月より現職。

　東京大学講師、東京理科大学講師、神奈川大学中小企業経営経理研究所客員教授を歴任。「税務から離れるな、税務にこだわるな」をモットーに、自身の強味である専門知識、執筆力、話術を活かし、税務・経営戦略などの分野で精力的に執筆活動をしている。近著に『経営ノート2017』『Enterpreneurship 101 ／失敗から学ぶ起業学入門」(共に東峰書房) ほか著書多数。

<Author Profile>
Yoshihiro Hongo
Certified Public Accountant & Licensed Tax Accountant

Current Chairman of Hongo Tsuji Group. Former President of Hongo Tsuji Tax & Accounting.

Waseda University (Political Science)　　　　　　B.A.

Waseda University (Graduate School of Commerce)　　M.A.

Registered as Certified Public Accountant

After establishing Hongo Tsuji Tax & Consulting, Yoshihiro Hongo, as its President, expanded the firm to one comprised of 1,400 staff members, and services 10,000 clients.

As an accounting professional who worked in the accounting and tax fields for over 30 years, he has developed relationships with executives, entrepreneurs and other well-known figures in all types of industries.

He has been appointed Chairman since January, 2016.

He has held positions as Lecturer of the University of Tokyo and the Tokyo University of Science, as well as Professor of the Institute of Accounting Research at Kanagawa University.

He actively engages in writing activities in the areas of tax and management consulting to which he channels his strengths including his professional expertise, writing skills, and speech, based on the motto of "Do not avoid taxes, but do not dwell on them."

Recently, he wrote "Management Notes 2017," and "Enterpreneurship 101" (Both published by Tohoshobo), and has published many other books.

辻・本郷グループ

- 辻・本郷 税理士法人
- 辻・本郷 ビジネスコンサルティング株式会社
- 辻・本郷 ITコンサルティング株式会社
- Hongo Connect & Consulting株式会社
- CSアカウンティング株式会社
- 株式会社アルファステップ
- 辻・本郷 社会保険労務士法人
- 一般財団法人 辻・本郷 財産管理機構
- TH弁護士法人

　2002年4月設立の辻・本郷税理士法人を中核とした企業グループ。東京新宿に本部を置く。

　日本国内に58拠点、海外に7拠点、スタッフ総勢1400名、顧問先10000社の国内最大規模を誇る税理士法人としての業務にとどまらず、企業再生やM&A、事業承継、更には不動産業や保険業、医業コンサルティングやハンズオン投資など多角的に事業展開する。

　顧客の立場に立ったワンストップサービスとあらゆるニーズに応える総合力をもって多岐にわたる業務展開をしている。

辻・本郷グループ（辻・本郷 税理士法人）

〒160-0022
東京都新宿区新宿4丁目1番6号　JR新宿ミライナタワー 28階
電話　03-5323-3301（代）
FAX　03-5323-3302
URL　http://www.ht-tax.or.jp/

Hongo Tsuji Group

- Hongo Tsuji Tax & Accounting
- Hongo Tsuji Business Consulting Co., Ltd.
- Hongo Tsuji IT Consulting Co., Ltd.
- Hongo Connect & Consulting Co., Ltd.
- CS Accounting Co., Ltd.
- Alpha Step Co., Ltd.
- Hongo Tsuji Social & Labor Insurance Co., Ltd.
- Hongo Tsuji Asset Management (General Incorporated Foundation)
- TH Law Corporation

The head office is located in Shinjuku, Tokyo, centered upon Tsuji Hongo Tax & Accounting, which was established in April, 2002.

The firm is the largest accounting firm in Japan which not only has 58 offices in Japan domestically, 7 offices overseas, 1400 staff members, and 10,000 client, but is also expanding multilaterally in the areas of corporate restructuring, M&A, business succession, real estate, insurance, medical consultation, and hands-on investment.

The firm is expanding its business in various areas with its ability to provide a one-stop service that accords with client needs, and with its comprehensive power that is able to meet different needs.

Hongo Tsuji Group (Hongo Tsuji Tax & Accounting)

JR SHINJUKU MIRAINA TOWER 28F 4-1-6, Shinjuku, Shinjuku-ku, Tokyo, 160-0022, Japan

TEL +81-3-5323-3301
FAX +81-3-5323-3302
URL http://www.ht-tax.or.jp/

資産を作る! 資産を防衛する!

2017年8月2日 初版第1刷発行

著者	本郷孔洋
発行者	鏡渕 敬
発行所	株式会社 東峰書房
	〒102-0074 東京都千代田区九段南4-2-12
	電話　03-3261-3136　FAX　03-3261-3185
	http://tohoshobo.info/
装幀・デザイン	小谷中一愛
イラスト	道端知美
印刷・製本	株式会社 シナノパブリッシングプレス

©Yoshihiro Hongo　2017
ISBN 978-4-88592-188-9 C0034

Make assets! Defend your assets!

Publication Date : August 2, 2017

Author	Yoshihiro Hongo
Publisher	Kei Kagamifuchi
Publishing Office	TOHOSHOBO INC.
	4-2-12 Kudanminami, Chiyodaku, Tokyo, 102-0074 Japan
	Tel: +81-3-3261-3136 Fax: +81-3-3261-3185
	http://tohoshobo.info/
Binding and Design	Kadua Koyanaka
Illustration	Tomomi Michibata
Printer	Shinano Publishing Press Co.,Ltd.

© Yoshihiro Hongo　2017
ISBN 978-4-88592-188-9 C0034

[東峰書房 × 本郷孔洋の書籍]

本郷孔洋の経営ノート

本郷孔洋の経営ノート2011
～今を乗り切るヒント集～
本体1400円+(税)　ISBN:9784885921254

本郷孔洋の経営ノート2012
～会社とトップの戦略的跳び方～
本体1600円+(税)　ISBN:9784885921353

本郷孔洋の経営ノート2013
～残存者利益を取りに行け！～
本体1400円+(税)　ISBN:9784885921490

本郷孔洋の経営ノート2014
～資産防衛の経営～
本体1400円+(税)　ISBN:9784885921629

本郷孔洋の経営ノート2015
～3年で勝負が決まる!～
本体1400円+(税)　ISBN:9784885921667

本郷孔洋の経営ノート2016
～常識の真逆は、ブルーオーシャン～
本体1400円+(税)　ISBN:9784885921766

本郷孔洋の経営ノート2017
～大航海時代のビジネスチャンス～
本体1400円+(税)　ISBN:9784885921865

環境ビジネス

「環境ビジネス」があしたを創る
~地球温暖化・CO_2・水問題で私たちができること~
本体1500円+(税)　ISBN:9784885920899

続「環境ビジネス」があしたを創る
~太陽経済の誕生か?~
本体1500円+(税)　ISBN:9784885921513

続々「環境ビジネス」があしたを創る
~黄金の10年がやってくる~
本体1500円+(税)　ISBN:9784885921650

私の起業ものがたり
本体1400円+(税)　ISBN:9784885921612

部下に贈る99の言葉
~本郷理事長が全社員に送ったメッセージ~
本体1400円+(税)　ISBN:9784885921520

経営書から学んだ経営
~顧問先10000社の公認会計士が読んでいる経営書~
本体1400円+(税)　ISBN:9784885921711

Entrepreneurship 101
失敗から学ぶ起業学入門
本体1500円+(税)　ISBN:9784885921827

日英2カ国語併記